**DATE DUE**

| | | | |
|---|---|---|---|
| | | | |
| | | | |
| | | | |
| | | | |
| | | | |
| | | | |
| | | | |
| | | | |
| | | | |
| | | | |
| | | | |
| | | | |
| | | | |

AMERICAN VOICES FROM

# The Vietnam Era

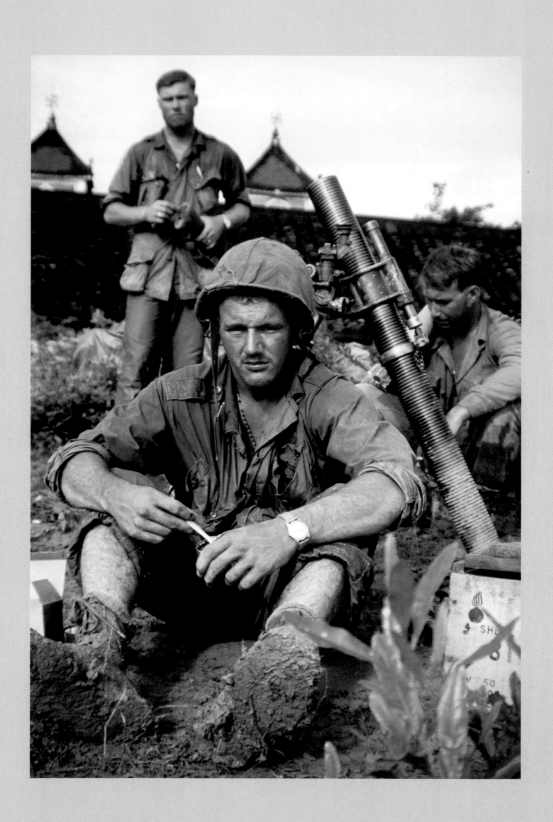

AMERICAN VOICES FROM

# The Vietnam Era

Virginia Schomp

BENCHMARK BOOKS

MARSHALL CAVENDISH
NEW YORK

# TO THE VETERANS,
## with thanks

Benchmark Books
Marshall Cavendish
99 White Plains Road
Tarrytown, New York 10591-9001
www.marshallcavendish.com

Text copyright © 2005 by Marshall Cavendish Corporation
Map copyright © 2005 by Marshall Cavendish Corporation
Map by Laszlo Kubinyi

All Internet sites were available and accurate when sent to press.

*Library of Congress Cataloging-in-Publication Data*
Schomp, Virginia.
The Vietnam era / by Virginia Schomp.
p. cm. — (American voices from—)
Summary: Describes, through excerpts from diaries, speeches, newspaper articles,
and other documents of the time, the Vietnam War and related events that occurred in
the United States during the 1960's, including the women's movement, the struggle
for civil rights, and the generation gap. Includes review questions.
Includes bibliographical references and index.
ISBN 0-7614-1693-5
1. Vietnamese Conflict, 1961–1975—United States—Juvenile literature.
2. United States—History—1961–1975—Juvenile literature. 3. United States—History—
1969—Juvenile literature. [1. Vietnamese Conflict, 1961–1975—United States—Sources.
2. United States—History—1961–1975—Sources.] I. Title. II. Series.
DS558.S359 2003      973.923—dc21
2003001475

Printed in China
1 3 5 6 4 2

Series design and composition by Anne Scatto / PIXEL PRESS
Art Research by Rose Corbett Gordon, Mystic CT

*The photographs in this book are used by permission and through the courtesy of:*

Cover: Wally McNamee/CORBIS
Bettmann/Corbis: pages ii, iix, xxiv, 36, 39, 42, 63, 82, 94, 124 & 127
Army Art Collection, U.S, Army Center of Military History: page x
David J. & Janice L. Frent Collection/Corbis: page xii
Lyndon Baines Johnson Library: pages xx & 101
Reuters NewMedia Inc./Corbis: page xxiii
AP/Wide World Photos: pages xiv, 8, 17, 20, 34, 68, 72, 75, 80, 91, 97, 110, 119 & 120

Marilyn Silverstone/Magnum: page 13
Wally McNamee/CORBIS: page 25
Paul Fusco/Magnum: page 48
Bob Adelman/Magnum: page 53
Eve Arnold/Magnum: page 57
Elliott Landy/Magnum: page 66
From Emery: *Watergate: The Corruption of American Politics and the Fall of Richard Nixon*: page 108
Leif Skoogfors/Corbis: page 122

ON THE COVER: Vietnam combat veterans at an antiwar rally in Washington, D.C., in May 1971.

ON THE TITLE PAGE: U.S. Army infantrymen on a search-and-destroy mission in South Vietnam take a break to rest and eat.

# Acknowledgments

"Peter Arnett Joins American Forces under Fire" from "The Agony and Death of Supply Column 21" by Peter Arnett, August 19, 1965. Reprinted with permission of The Associated Press.

"The *Washington Daily News* Reacts to Tet" from the *Washington Daily News,* January 31, 1968. Reprinted with permission by The Washington Post.

"A Photographer Records an Assassination" from Al Santoli, *To Bear Any Burden.* New York: E. P. Dutton, 1985. Reprinted by permission of Al Santoli.

"Walter Cronkite Reports from Vietnam" from "CBS News Special: Walter Cronkite's Report from Vietnam (Who, What, When, Where, Why)," February 27, 1968. Reprinted by permission of CBS News Archives.

"A Grunt Patrols the Jungle," "A Bitter Soldier Asks 'Why?'" "A GI Explains the War to American Schoolchildren," and "Servicemen React to Protests at Home" originally appeared in *Dear America: Letters Home from Vietnam,* edited by Bernard Edelman for the New York Vietnam Veterans Memorial Commission. Published by W. W. Norton & Company, 1985, 2002. Reprinted by permission of Bernard Edelman.

"Tim O'Brien Walks through a Mine Field" from Tim O'Brien, *If I Die in a Combat Zone,* New York: Delacorte Press, 1973. Reprinted by permission of Dell Publishing, a division of Random House.

"A Veteran-Poet Reflects on 'Guerrilla War'" from *Vietnam: A Television History,* Boston: WGBH Educational Foundation, 1983; poem from W. D. Ehrhart, *Beautiful Wreckage: New & Selected Poems by W. D. Ehrhart,* Easthampton, MA: Adastra Press, 1999. Reprinted by permission of W. D. Ehrhart.

"A Reporter Runs with Rioters in Chicago" from John Hohenberg, editor, *The Pulitzer Prize Story II, 1959–1980,* © 1980 Columbia University Press. Reprinted with the permission of the publisher.

"College Graduates See a Future without Hope" from the *Brown Daily Herald,* June 2, 1968. Reprinted with the permission of the publisher.

"David Obst Remembers the 'People's Park'" from David Obst, *Too Good to Be Forgotten,* copyright © 1998. Reprinted by permission of John Wiley & Sons, Inc.

"Country Joe McDonald Sings at Woodstock" from "I-Feel-Like-I'm-Fixin'-to-Die-Rag," lyrics by Joe McDonald, © 1965 renewed 1993 by Alkatraz Corner Music. Used by permission.

"Malcolm X Speaks Out against Integration" from *The Autobiography of Malcolm X* by Malcolm X and Alex Haley, copyright © 1964 by Alex Haley and Malcolm X. Copyright © 1965 by Alex Haley and Betty Shabazz. Used by permission of Arlington House, a division of Random House, Inc.

"A Black Veteran Recalls Racial Tensions in the Infantry" from *Bloods: An Oral History of the Vietnam War by Black Veterans* by Wallace Terry, copyright © 1984 by Wallace Terry. Used by permission of Arlington House, a division of Random House, Inc.

"Phyllis Schlafly Defines a Successful Marriage" from Phyllis Schlafly, *The Power of the Positive Woman,* copyright © 1977 by Phyllis Schlafly. Used by permission of Arlington House, a division of Random House, Inc.

"A GI Sets the Scene for the My Lai Massacre" from Seymour M. Hersh, *My Lai 4: A Report on the Massacre and Its Aftermath.* New York: Random House, 1970. Reprinted by permission of Seymour Hersh.

"The *New York Times* Defends Publication of the Pentagon Papers" from "The Vietnam Documents," *New York Times,* June 16, 1971. Reprinted by permission of the *New York Times.*

"*Doonesbury* Draws on Watergate," Doonesbury © 1973 G. B. Trudeau. Reprinted with permission of UNIVERSAL PRESS SYNDICATE.

"Three Servicemen Return Home from Vietnam" from Bob Greene, *Homecoming: When the Soldiers Returned from Vietnam.* New York: G. P. Putnam's, 1989.

"A Washington Memorial Honors Vietnam Veterans" from *Shrapnel in the Heart: Letters and Remembrances from the Vietnam Veterans Memorial* by Laura Palmer, © 1987 by Laura Palmer, Random House. Reprinted courtesy of Random House.

# Contents

About Primary Sources ... ix
Introduction: America's Longest War ... xv
Map: Vietnam before 1975 ... xvii

Chapter 1 | A Television War ... 1

Peter Arnett Joins American Forces under Fire ... 3
The *Washington Daily News* Reacts to Tet ... 6
A Photographer Records an Assassination ... 7
Walter Cronkite Reports from Vietnam ... 10

Chapter 2 | The Unseen Enemy ... 12

A Grunt Patrols the Jungle ... 15
Tim O'Brien Walks through a Mine Field ... 18
A Marine Writes from the Trenches of Khe Sanh ... 20
A Veteran-Poet Reflects on "Guerrilla War" ... 22

Chapter 3 | The War at Home: "Doves" for Peace ... 24

A Bitter Soldier Asks "Why?" ... 27
An Antiwar Petition Opposes the "Crime of Silence" ... 29
A Reporter Runs with Rioters in Chicago ... 31
The *Akron Beacon Journal* Covers a Tragedy at Kent State ... 35

Chapter 4 | The War at Home: "Hawks" for War ... 38

President Johnson Explains Why America Is in Vietnam ... 40
A GI Explains the War to American Schoolchildren ... 43
President Nixon Appeals to the "Silent Majority" ... 44
A Member of the "Silent Majority" Speaks ... 47
Servicemen React to Protests at Home ... 49

Chapter 5 | American Youth and the Counterculture ... 52

SDS Explains Why Youth Are Alienated ... 55
College Graduates See a Future without Hope ... 58
David Obst Remembers the "People's Park" ... 60

A *Life* Poll Examines the Generation Gap  62
Country Joe McDonald Sings at Woodstock  64

Chapter 6  |  The Battle for Civil Rights                      69

Martin Luther King Opposes the Vietnam War  71
Malcolm X Speaks Out against Integration  73
The Black Panthers Give a Lesson in Politics  75
Mississippi Activists Say Blacks Should Refuse to Serve in Vietnam  78
A Black Veteran Recalls Racial Tensions in the Infantry  80

Chapter 7  |  The Women's Liberation Movement                 83

Florynce Kennedy Talks to *Life* about the Women's Movement  85
Congress Passes the Equal Rights Amendment  87
Gloria Steinem Defends the ERA  88
Phyllis Schlafly Defines a Successful Marriage  90
Rose Sandecki Serves in Vietnam  92

Chapter 8  |  The Credibility Gap                             96

President Johnson Sees No "Way of Winning" in Vietnam  99
A GI Sets the Scene for the My Lai Massacre  102
The *New York Times* Defends Publication of the Pentagon Papers  104
President Nixon Wields a "Smoking Gun"  106
*Doonesbury* Draws on Watergate  108

Chapter 9  |  Coming Home                                    111

Three Servicemen Return Home from Vietnam  113
The Paris Peace Accords End U.S. Involvement in Vietnam  115
A Navy Captain Describes the Evacuation of Saigon  118
A Washington Memorial Honors Vietnam Veterans  121

Time Line                                                    124
Glossary                                                     128
To Find Out More                                             130
Index                                                        132

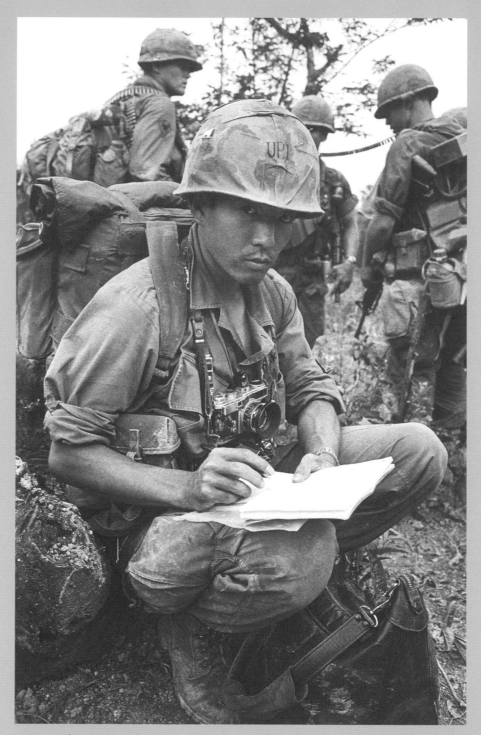

A journalist covers the war in Vietnam. More than 400 war correspondents from 22 nations shared danger with the combat soldiers to report stories from the battlefront. Their firsthand accounts are some of our most important primary sources on American involvement in Vietnam.

# About Primary Sources

## What Is a Primary Source?

In the pages that follow, you will be hearing many different "voices" from a special time in America's past. Some of the selections are long and others are short. You'll find many easy to understand at first reading, while others may require several readings. All the selections have one thing in common, however. They are primary sources. This is the name historians give to the bits and pieces of information that make up the record of human existence. Primary sources are important to us because they are the core material of all historical investigation. You might call them "history" itself.

Primary sources are evidence; they give historians the all-important clues they need to understand the past. Perhaps you have read a detective story in which a sleuth must solve a mystery by piecing together bits of evidence he or she uncovers. The detective makes deductions, or educated guesses based on the evidence, and solves the mystery once all the deductions point in a certain

A soldier-artist painted this scene of fellow GIs catching a nap on a military plane.

direction. Historians work in much the same way. Like detectives, historians analyze data through careful reading and rereading. After much analysis, they draw conclusions about an event, a person, or an entire era. Different historians may analyze the same evidence and come to different conclusions. That is why there is often sharp disagreement about an event.

Primary sources are also called documents. This rather dry word can be used to describe many different things: an official speech by a government leader, an old map, an act of Congress, a letter worn out from much handling, an entry hastily scrawled in a diary, a detailed newspaper account of an event, a funny or sad song, a colorful poster, a cartoon, a faded photograph, or someone's remembrances captured on tape or film.

By examining the following documents, you the reader will be taking on the role of historian. Here is your chance to immerse yourself in a turbulent era in recent American history—the two decades of U.S. military involvement in Vietnam. You'll come to know the men and women who served in that controversial war and the leaders who shaped government policy. You'll meet "hawks" and "doves"—Americans who supported the war and those who marched in protest against it. You'll read the words of African Americans fighting for civil rights, women struggling for equality, and younger and older Americans on both sides of the "generation gap."

## How to Read a Primary Source

Each document in this book comes from the period of American involvement in Vietnam in the 1960s and 1970s. Some are the official papers of presidents and other major figures in American history. Others are taken from war correspondents' accounts printed in newspapers or broadcast on television. There are letters and recollections by servicemen and women in Vietnam as well as people participating in the struggles and upheavals on the American home front. All of the documents help us to understand what it was like to live during the Vietnam era.

As you read each document, ask yourself some basic questions. Who is writing or speaking? Who is that person's audience? What is the writer's point of view? What is he or she trying to tell the audience? Is the message clearly expressed, or is it implied, that is, stated indirectly? What words does the writer use to convey his or

One of the most notable features of the Vietnam era was the widespread antiwar movement. These buttons are evidence of the many different antiwar organizations and protest rallies.

her message? Are the words emotional or objective in tone? If you are looking at a photograph, examine it carefully, taking in all the details. Where do you think it was taken? What is happening in the foreground? In the background? Is it posed or an action shot? How can you tell? Who do you think took the picture, and what is its purpose? These are questions that can help you think critically about a primary source.

Some tools have been included with the documents to help you in your investigations. Unusual words have been listed and defined near the selections. Thought-provoking questions follow each document. They help focus your reading so you can get the most out of the document. As you read each selection, you'll probably come up with many questions of your own. That's great! The work of a historian always leads to many, many questions. Some can be answered, while others require more investigation. Perhaps when you finish this book, your questions will lead you to further explorations of the Vietnam era.

In the Vietnam era many "baby boomers" rejected the older generation's lifestyle and values. Long hair and blue jeans became symbols of youthful rebellion, as seen in this photograph from the Haight-Ashbury district of San Francisco, a center of the "hippie" movement.

# Introduction

# AMERICA'S LONGEST WAR

In the early 1960s the United States and Vietnam were worlds apart, not just geographically but in the politics, prosperity, history, and hopes of their peoples.

The United States was a giant. It had emerged from World War II in 1945 as the most powerful nation in the world, with the largest military force and the strongest economy. After the war its economy continued to grow. Americans were better off than ever before, enjoying good jobs and rising incomes. Millions bought their first homes and filled them with the consumer goods pouring out of American factories, including new "modern conveniences" such as television sets, automatic washers and dryers, and electric dishwashers.

Postwar prosperity also led to a "baby boom." Children were born in record numbers in the peaceful, plentiful years following World War II, and they grew up sharing their parents' pride and confidence in the American democratic, capitalist system. They believed there was no limit to what their great nation could do. And, like their parents, they were passionately anticommunist.

Since World War II's end, rivalry between the United States and the Communist Soviet Union had developed into a "cold war," with distrust and hostility on each side. U.S. leaders, convinced that communism was the most serious threat to the American way of life, vowed to combat the spread of the "red menace" before the "Commies" took over the world.

Compared to America, Vietnam was just a dot on the map. But this small nation in the southeast corner of Asia had a long and rich history. Founded more than two thousand years ago, Vietnam had struggled throughout its existence against one foreign power and then another. China, its mammoth neighbor to the north, ruled the tiny country for more than a thousand years, until Vietnam won its independence in 938. Over the next nine hundred years, the Vietnamese fought off frequent attacks by Chinese and Mongol forces. Then, in the nineteenth century, as European powers set up colonial empires throughout Asia, Vietnam was occupied by France.

The French were harsh rulers who stripped the land of its natural resources and taxed the people into desperate poverty. In the 1940s Vietnamese Communist leader Ho Chi Minh organized a revolutionary force, the Viet Minh, to fight for independence. Ho and his followers waged a guerrilla war, using small groups in ambushes, sabotage, and swift hit-and-run raids. Gradually they wore down their much better armed opponents. In 1954, after a seven-week battle in the valley of Dien Bien Phu, the Communist Viet Minh drove the French out of Vietnam. Peace talks were held in Geneva, Switzerland. The Geneva peace agreement temporarily divided Vietnam in two, with the north ruled by Ho Chi Minh's Communists from their capital at Hanoi and the south by non-

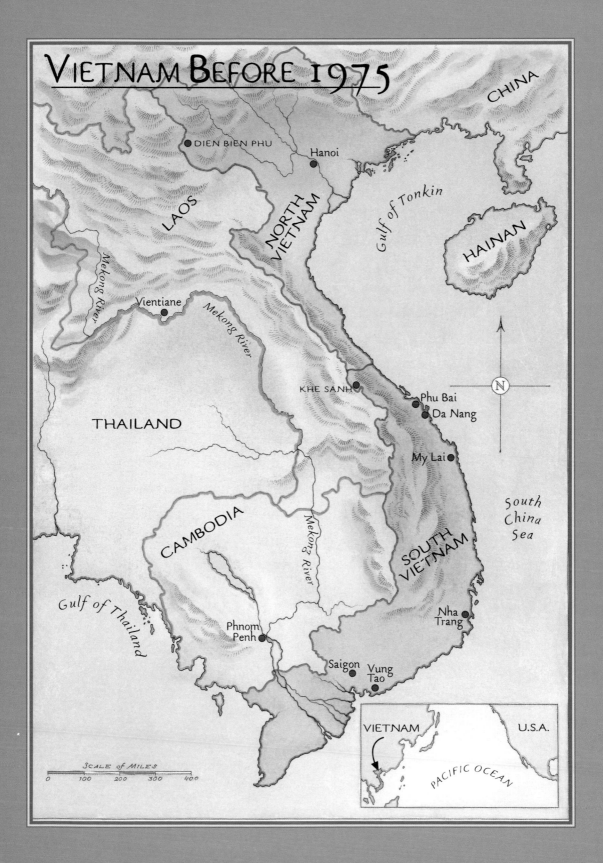

# VIETNAM BEFORE 1975

CHINA

DIEN BIEN PHU

Hanoi

LAOS

NORTH VIETNAM

Gulf of Tonkin

HAINAN

Mekong River

Vientiane

Mekong River

THAILAND

KHE SANH

Phu Bai

Da Nang

My Lai

South China Sea

CAMBODIA

Mekong River

SOUTH VIETNAM

Gulf of Thailand

Nha Trang

Phnom Penh

Saigon

Vung Tao

N

SCALE of MILES

0   100   200   300   400

VIETNAM                          U.S.A.

PACIFIC OCEAN

Communists based at Saigon. Elections were scheduled for 1956, when the Vietnamese would choose a single leader and reunite the country under one government.

U.S. leaders denounced the Geneva agreement. They were afraid the Communists would take over all of Vietnam and, if that happened, the other countries of Southeast Asia would fall to communism one by one, like a row of dominoes. President Dwight Eisenhower decided to support Ngo Dinh Diem, leader of the anti-Communist forces. Eisenhower sent money and war supplies, along with nine hundred military advisers to train Diem's Army of the Republic of Vietnam (ARVN). Determined to hold on to power, Diem announced that he would not participate in nationwide elections. Instead, he held his own rigged election and proclaimed himself president of South Vietnam.

In 1960 John F. Kennedy succeeded Eisenhower as U.S. president. Kennedy believed in the "domino theory" and pledged to "pay any price, bear any burden" to halt the spread of communism. He poured money and equipment into South Vietnam and increased the number of U.S. military advisers to more than 16,000. But it soon became apparent that President Diem could not hold out against the Communists. His government was hopelessly inefficient and corrupt. He placed relatives in all the top posts, favored the rich, oppressed the poor, and used secret police to brutally suppress all opposition. Diem's policies made him so unpopular that many South Vietnamese turned against him to support Ho Chi Minh.

Ho was just as ruthless as Diem. The Communist government in North Vietnam was a dictatorship that tightly controlled the schools and newspapers, outlawed all opposition political parties, and executed thousands of non-Communists and "reactionaries"—anyone suspected of disagreeing with its policies. But unlike Diem, Ho knew how to win the support of the people. His followers went from village to village, helping the poor, promising land, and stirring up anger against Diem's repressive rule. The Communists urged villagers to support their struggle for a free, united Vietnam and painted South Vietnam's American allies as just the latest in a long history of foreign invaders.

Thousands of Viet Minh fighters had fled north when the country was divided. Now they slipped back into South Vietnam, joining other Communist supporters in a new guerrilla organization known as the Vietcong. The guerrillas assassinated South Vietnamese government officials and attacked ARVN posts. By the fall of 1963, they had become so powerful—and the opposition to the Saigon government was so widespread—that U.S. leaders decided it was time for Diem to go. President Kennedy secretly approved a plot by ARVN generals to overthrow the South Vietnamese president. During the takeover, Diem was murdered. Three weeks later, Kennedy himself was assassinated in Dallas, Texas, and the growing nightmare of U.S. involvement in Vietnam passed to a new president.

President Lyndon Johnson had strongly supported Kennedy's policies in Vietnam. He too believed that the Communists were a threat to America and the rest of the free world, and he felt duty bound to honor the commitments made by U.S. presidents before him. But the situation in Vietnam was rapidly deteriorating. The series of generals who had taken power after Diem's overthrow had all proven equally incompetent. The Vietcong, aided by soldiers of the North Vietnamese Army (NVA), were winning the war in the south. Johnson increased U.S. aid. He also approved secret operations that included sending U.S. Navy ships to the Tonkin Gulf, off the North Vietnamese coast, to spy on NVA military bases. In August 1964 one of those ships reported that it had been fired on by enemy patrol boats. The report was confusing and probably wrong. Nevertheless, Johnson used it to persuade Congress to grant him authority to widen the war. The Tonkin Gulf Resolution gave the president unlimited power "to prevent further aggression" in Southeast Asia.

President Lyndon Johnson is overcome with emotion after listening to reports from the battlefields in Vietnam. The unpopular war crippled Johnson's programs for social reform and eventually ended his political career.

On March 2, 1965, President Johnson ordered the start of Operation Rolling

Thunder, a massive bombing campaign against military targets in North Vietnam. A week later, he sent in 3,500 marines—the first U.S. combat troops in Vietnam. For the rest of Johnson's administration, the "Americanization" of the war continued, with the bombings intensifying and increasing numbers of soldiers arriving to support those already in the country. War had never been formally declared. Many Americans did not believe their country's military forces should be involved in Southeast Asia. Nevertheless, by the end of 1968, there were more than 536,000 U.S. troops in Vietnam, and more than 30,000 Americans had been killed in action. Step by step, the United States had stumbled into the most controversial war in its history.

In 1968 Richard Nixon was elected president. By now Congress and a majority of the American people had turned against the Vietnam War. The new president promised to achieve "peace with honor"—ending U.S. involvement while honoring the commitments made to South Vietnam—through a policy called Vietnamization. Nixon would gradually withdraw U.S. combat troops while providing massive amounts of money, weapons, and training to strengthen South Vietnam's army so it could fight and win on its own. By March 1972, only 95,000 American troops remained in Vietnam, and the ARVN had become one of the best-supplied armies in the world. But Vietnamization was a failure. Although ARVN soldiers sometimes fought with great courage, their leaders were weak and corrupt, concerned more about wealth and political standing than military matters. Meanwhile, the Communists were determined to fight as long as it took, suffering unlimited casualties, to attain "final victory."

Peace negotiations between the warring parties had begun in Paris in 1968 and continued off and on throughout the war. In January 1973 the negotiators reached a settlement. The Paris Peace Accords called for a truce, with each side holding on to the lands it already occupied. The United States would withdraw its remaining forces, and an international commission would be set up to work toward permanent peace. Almost immediately, both Vietnams violated the agreement. NVA troops poured into the south, preparing for a final offensive. In early 1975 they overran South Vietnam, capturing one city after another. On April 30, 1975, the Vietnam War ended when the last Americans were evacuated from the roof of the U.S. Embassy as NVA troops stormed into Saigon.

The long years of U.S. involvement in Vietnam had dramatic repercussions on the American home front. Doubts about government policy grew into the largest antiwar movement in American history. Clashes between antiwar doves and prowar hawks became increasingly angry, sometimes leading to violence. These confrontations played out against a background of other conflicts threatening to tear the country apart. African Americans who demanded their civil rights faced arrests, beatings, and murder, while race riots rocked city ghettoes. Young people who were disillusioned with American society rebelled, shocking the older generation with their long hair, rock-and-roll music, and experiments with nontraditional lifestyles. Feminists called for "women's liberation" in a man's world. The Watergate scandal, with its revelations of lies and deceptions reaching all the way to the president's office, shook Americans' faith and confidence in their government.

A student throws a tear-gas canister back at police during a college antiwar protest.

All these social and political forces made the Vietnam era a time of great energy, upheaval, and change. Listening to the voices of Americans who lived through those turbulent times—both on the battlefront and the home front—can give us a better understanding of how past events unfolded and how they helped shape the world we live in today.

A South Vietnamese mother and her children flee an American bombing raid on their village. The raid was made to root out Vietcong snipers who were firing on U.S. Marines, and the villagers were warned of the attack before it began.

# Chapter I

# A Television War

**V**IETNAM HAS BEEN CALLED America's first television war. Since the end of the Korean War in 1953, nearly every U.S. household had acquired that new technological marvel, the TV set. Now families tuning in to their favorite nightly news show could see young American soldiers under enemy fire, falling wounded, lined up in mute rows of body bags. They watched U.S. Marines setting fire to Vietnamese villages, women weeping, children running from artillery fire. War is always brutal and ugly, but this was the first time television brought war's grim realities right into Americans' living rooms. Most people did not like what they saw.

For all of television's immediacy and emotional impact, the picture it presented wasn't always accurate. The business of television is entertainment. Reporters and film editors must grab the viewer's attention with powerful images and compress complicated events into a two- or three-minute story. A Vietnamese farmer plowing his fields or a GI resting up in base camp doesn't make good television; firefights and burning villages do. By focusing on the high points of drama and conflict, TV can make the unusual seem standard. As one journalist has noted, "It is probable that a regular viewer [of TV news] saw more infantry action over a longer span of days than most of the American troops who were in Vietnam."

Along with the disturbing images bombarding them from their TV sets, Americans experienced the war through the graphic photographs and descriptions of battle in their daily newspapers. During World War II and the Korean War, journalists had been required to submit their writings to military censors, who made sure nothing was published that could aid the enemy or damage morale back home. In the undeclared war in Vietnam, however, there was no military censorship. Journalists agreed to follow a set of voluntary guidelines that forbade the spreading of information that might threaten military security, such as troop movements. Otherwise, they were free to go wherever they wished and report whatever they pleased, no matter how shocking or controversial.

Critics of the media have argued that television and newspaper coverage of the Vietnam War contributed to the U.S. defeat. They claim that the distorted and violent images on TV, along with negative reporting by antiwar correspondents, turned the American public against the war and eventually forced the United States to withdraw from Vietnam. On the other side, media defenders note that most correspondents supported the government position throughout much of the Vietnam War. Reporting did not become overwhelmingly negative until late in 1968, when increasing numbers of Americans began to oppose the war. In this point of view, the media did not shape public opinion but simply reflected it.

Which of these views is correct? As with most controversies, there is no simple answer. While you are reading the following reports by Vietnam-era correspondents, you may want to keep this question in mind and draw your own conclusions.

## Peter Arnett Joins American Forces under Fire

Peter Arnett of the Associated Press (AP) went to Vietnam in 1962 and remained through the evacuation of Saigon in 1975. A respected journalist who won the Pulitzer Prize for International Correspondence in 1966, he routinely risked his life under fire to cover the news. Arnett wrote this account of one of the first engagements of the war involving U.S. combat troops after he and a photographer

*"Survivors said the Vietcong rose out of hedge rows and swamps."*

hopped off an army cargo helicopter that had mistakenly landed right in the heart of the action. The story of Supply Column 21 appeared in American newspapers on August 19, 1965. U.S. Marine commanders, who had been claiming glorious victories in Vietnam, responded to Arnett's account of the American defeat by denying that the battle had taken place. The marines continued their denials for several months, until the AP produced photographs of the engagement that forced them to admit the story was true.

VAN TUONG, Vietnam (AP)—The mission of U.S. Marine Supply Column 21 yesterday was simple: Get to the beachhead, resupply a line company and return to the 7th Fleet mother ship anchored a mile out in the bay.

**line company**
*a combat unit*

It never found the line company. And it never returned.

Supply Column 21 was a formidable force made up of five steel-shod amtraks—35-ton amphibious vehicles—to carry food and ammunition—and two M 48 tanks to escort them once ashore.

The column packed a total of 287 tons of steel. It was made up of 30 men.

The paths that led to its destruction were paved with confusion.

Failing to locate the designated line company immediately, Column 21 set out to look for it.

But the huge amtraks, once out of the water, were unwieldy. They flopped from one rice paddy to another, with their crews [stopping] at one battalion and then the next. No one seemed to pay much attention.

At 11 A.M., Supply Column 21 was about 400 yards ahead of the nearest Marine [company]. The vehicles were deep in Vietcong territory and, suddenly, were deep in trouble.

Survivors said the Vietcong rose out of hedge rows and swamps.

Lance Corporal Richard Pass of Homewood, Ill., said his amtrak veered aside as explosions erupted around them. The leading tank was hit with an armor-piercing shell. Two men inside were wounded.

The terraced paddies made maneuvering difficult and the supply men were not trained for it. Attempting to get in to good firing positions, three of the five amtraks backed into a deep paddy and bogged down.

The other two edged toward the tanks for shelter. One didn't make it. A Vietcong knocked it out by dropping a grenade down its hatch, killing two Americans inside and wounding others.

Mortar fire bounced off the vehicles and cannon put three holes in one tank. The wounded driver squeezed himself through the 18-inch wide escape hatch under his vehicle only to be riddled by bullets.

Corporal Pass saw Vietcong with ammunition bandoliers, black pajama uniforms, and camouflaged steel helmets move right up to an amtrak 30 yards to his left.

He said the doors of the vehicle clanged open as the two drivers tried to make a break to Pass's vehicle. One of the Americans was killed as he leaped out.

The other was plunging through the paddyfield swinging his Marine knife when he went down. When pulled out dead today, he still had the knife clutched in his hand.

Soon after noon, as the hot sun beat down on the scurrying figures and the steel vehicles, the Vietcong knocked out a third amtrak. Survivors massed in the other two. . . .

In late afternoon, air strikes eased the pressure.

By this time, a lieutenant had been killed and another wounded.

Another tank joined the beleaguered group.

At daybreak, a solitary helicopter landed at the scene. It had mistaken the landing zone.

At the drone of the helicopter, the Americans surged from their amtraks like moths to a flame.

Crouched, and with weapons at the ready, the Americans slipped past the bodies of their own and the enemy. They carried the wounded to the helicopter and left the dead.

The helicopter came back once for more wounded. . . .

The fate of Supply Column 21 was sealed at noon.

The men thought the disabled vehicles might be carted off and repaired. But an officer of the relief force told them:

"Take your personal belongings out of the vehicles. We're going to blow them up."

The remains of the amtraks at Van Tuong will be a reminder of Supply Column 21.

—From Peter Arnett, "The Agony and Death of Supply Column 21,"
Associated Press, August 19, 1965.

## THINK ABOUT THIS

**1.** Why do you think the military tried to deny Arnett's story?

**2.** How might accounts like this affect readers' opinions about the war and American military leaders?

# The *Washington Daily News* Reacts to Tet

In early 1968 the Tet Offensive marked a turning point in the Vietnam War. Military leaders, responding to growing doubts and impatience on the American home front, had been proclaiming that the war was nearly won and peace was "just around the corner." Then, on the night of January 30, the beginning of the Vietnamese New Year holiday called Tet, North Vietnamese and Vietcong soldiers launched a massive surprise attack on cities throughout South Vietnam. For weeks U.S. and South Vietnamese forces battled the Communists. In the end they were victorious, retaking the cities and killing more than 40,000 enemy troops. But to the American public, Tet looked like anything but a victory. TV images of savage house-to-house fighting, bodies littering the floors of the U.S. Embassy in Saigon, and ancient cities reduced to rubble sent shock waves across the United States. The editorial pages of newspapers like the *Washington Daily News,* formerly supportive of government policy, accused U.S. leaders of misleading the public and began to question America's course in Vietnam.

WHERE WERE WE? Where ARE We?

The bold, massive communist attacks yesterday on Saigon, eight provincial capitals and 30 or 40 lesser towns were a shocker.

American Military Police having to land on the roof of the U.S. Embassy in Saigon under fire to recapture the supposedly "guerilla-proof" building from communists who held it six hours! That scene alone is enough to force the Johnson Administration to stamp invalid its optimistic assessment the war is showing "continual and steady progress." . . .

The caption for the political cartoon accompanying this front-page story on the Tet Offensive quotes the commander of U.S. forces in Vietnam, General William Westmoreland. Weeks earlier Westmoreland had declared that America had "turned the corner" in Vietnam and victory was in sight.

Once again American hopes and expectations in Vietnam have been blasted by our costly bad habit of under-estimating our enemy and overestimating our ally. . . .

If this kind of Viet cong attack had occurred as the war's opener—a sort of Pearl Harbor—it would be easier to understand, and more forgivable. But the war has now been raging five years, and the U.S. has been on the scene in strength for nearly three years. Is this the sort of defeat we should be suffering when we have a half-million men on the ground, and our top officials, flown back from Saigon to report just two months ago, tell us things are going well?

—*From the* Washington Daily News,
*January 31, 1968.*

## THINK ABOUT THIS

1. What facts does the editorial writer use to explain why the Tet assault on Saigon was a "shocker"?
2. How does the cartoon reinforce the editorial's message?

## A Photographer Records an Assassination

One of the most shocking images of the Vietnam War came from the Tet Offensive. On February 1, 1968, a suspected Vietcong officer who had been captured in Saigon was executed in the street by General Nguyen Ngoc Loan, South Vietnam's national police chief. Associated Press photographer Eddie Adams captured the killing on film. The next day his photograph appeared in newspapers and television broadcasts around the globe. Viewers were outraged. The picture of a bound, unarmed man being shot in cold blood with an American pistol by an American ally seemed to illustrate the special ugliness of the Vietnam War. Here is Adams's account of the events surrounding his Pulitzer Prize-winning photograph.

WE SAW THE POLICE WALKING OUT of a building with this prisoner. His hands were tied and they were walking him down the street. So like any newsman, you photograph him in case he trips and falls or somebody takes a swing at him, until they load him on the wagon and drive off. It was just a routine thing.

We get to the corner of the street. And all of a sudden, out of nowhere, comes General Loan, the national police chief. I was about five feet away from him, and I see him reach for his pistol. I thought he was going to threaten the prisoner. So as quick as he brought his pistol up, I took a picture. But it turned out he shot him. And the speed of my shutter . . . the bullet hadn't left his head yet. It was just coming out the other end. There

People all over the world were horrified by this shocking photo of a South Vietnamese police chief executing a Vietcong suspect.

was no blood until he was on the ground—whoosh. That's when I turned my back and wouldn't take a picture. There's a limit, certain times you don't take pictures.

I thought absolutely nothing of it. He shot him, so what? Because people die in . . . war. And I just happened to be there this time. This is not an unusual occurrence. I could tell you lots of stories—heads being chopped off, all kinds of hairy stuff.

*"I just happened to be there and took the picture."*

And I didn't find this out until much later, but the prisoner who was killed had himself killed a police major who was one of Loan's best friends, and knifed his entire family. The wife, six kids . . . the whole family. When they captured this guy, I didn't know that. I just happened to be there and took the picture. And all of a sudden I destroy a guy's life. I'm talking about the general, not the Viet Cong—he would have gotten shot if I was there or not. . . .

I'm not saying what he did was right or wrong. But I ask, "If you were the general, and they killed your people and their children, how do you know what you would have done?"

I didn't know until a couple of days later when I started getting these playback reports from all over the world. The photo was all over the front pages. Full page in Germany, different newspapers all over the world and America. I had no idea. . . . But it was very one-sided. I didn't have a picture of that Viet Cong blowing away the family. It was very detrimental [damaging]—perfect propaganda for North Vietnam.

—From Al Santoli, To Bear Any Burden. *New York: E. P. Dutton, 1985.*

## THINK ABOUT THIS

1. We often accept photographs as the literal truth. How does Adams think they can be misleading or misinterpreted?
2. In Adams's opinion, what circumstances might have justified the execution? Do you agree with him? Why or why not?

# Walter Cronkite Reports from Vietnam

Walter Cronkite, anchor of the *CBS Evening News*, was perhaps the most trusted and respected American journalist of the Vietnam era. A supporter of U.S. government policy in Southeast Asia, Cronkite was deeply troubled by the news of the Tet Offensive. In February 1968 he traveled to Vietnam for a firsthand look. Returning home, Cronkite broadcast a special documentary on February 27 in which he delivered this personal editorial. He concluded that the war had become a costly stalemate that could not be won. Watching the broadcast, President Johnson exclaimed, "If I've lost Cronkite, I've lost middle America." Events seemed to prove the president right. Over the next few weeks, opinion polls showed a sharp drop in the American people's support for the war and for Johnson's handling of it. By the end of March, the president's approval ratings had slipped so low that he announced he would not seek reelection.

TONIGHT, BACK IN MORE FAMILIAR SURROUNDINGS in New York, we'd like to sum up our findings in Vietnam, an analysis that must be speculative, personal, subjective. Who won and who lost in the great Tet offensive against the cities? I'm not sure. The Vietcong did not win by a knockout, but neither did we. The referees of history may make it a draw. . . .

*"...with each escalation, the world comes closer to the brink of cosmic disaster."*

We have been too often disappointed by the optimism of the American leaders, both in Vietnam and Washington, to have faith any longer in the silver linings they find in the darkest clouds. They may be right, that Hanoi's winter-spring offensive has been forced by the communist realization that they could not win the longer war of attrition, and that the communists hope that any success in the offensive will improve their position for eventual negotiations. It would improve their position, and it would also require our realization, that we should have had all along, that any negotiations must be that—negotiations, not the dictation of peace terms. For it seems now more certain than ever that the bloody experience of Vietnam is to end in a stalemate. This summer's almost certain stand-off will either end in real give-and-take negotiations or terrible escalation; and for every means we have to escalate, the enemy can match us. . . . And with each escalation, the world comes closer to the brink of cosmic disaster.

To say that we are closer to victory today is to believe, in the face of the evidence, the optimists who have been wrong in the past. To suggest we are on the edge of defeat is to yield to unreasoning pessimism. To say that we are mired in stalemate seems the only realistic, yet unsatisfactory, conclusion. On the off chance that military and political analysts are right, in the next few months we must test the enemy's intentions, in case this is indeed his last gasp before negotiations. But it is increasingly clear to this reporter that the only rational way out then will be to negotiate, not as victors, but as an honorable people who lived up to their pledge to defend democracy, and did the best they could.

—From the "CBS News Special: Walter Cronkite's Report from Vietnam (Who, What, When, Where, Why)," February 27, 1968.

## THINK ABOUT THIS

1. What points does Cronkite make that support his conversion from a prowar to an antiwar position?

2. Cronkite is editorializing in the passage, giving his personal opinion on the war's future prospects and making recommendations on military policy. Do you think news broadcasters should express personal opinions such as these, or should they always present the news impartially? Would your answer change depending on the circumstances?

# Chapter 2

# The Unseen Enemy

**V**IETNAM WAS UNLIKE ANY WAR the United States had ever fought. In earlier wars soldiers had battled to capture and control territory, meeting the enemy in close combat on the front lines. In Vietnam it was nearly impossible to control territory. The Americans could drive the Vietcong from a village or hilltop one day only to find them slipping back in the next. Large battles were the exception, and there was no "front." Instead, the enemy could be almost anyone, almost anywhere.

The Vietcong were Vietnamese peasants. All the peasants, friend and enemy alike, spoke the same language and dressed in the same black cotton "pajamas." A farmer plowing his fields, a woman carrying her baby in a market basket, a base camp's cook or barber—all of these could be Vietcong sympathizers or guerrillas themselves. Even a young child might be trained to plant a time bomb or toss a grenade into a crowd of soldiers.

The American strategy in this baffling guerrilla war was called attrition—the gradual wearing down of the opponent through constant harassment and attacks. While U.S. bombers hammered the

A busy city street in South Vietnam. One of the greatest challenges
for American soldiers was telling which Vietnamese were
friendly and which secretly supported the Vietcong.

Communists in North Vietnam, ground forces carried out "search-and-destroy" missions in the South. The troops searched out Vietcong bases and supply areas and destroyed food, weapons, ammunition, and other supplies that might help the enemy. They tried to kill or capture the Vietcong and NVA soldiers. The goal was to keep up the pressure until the Communists gave in and gave up the fight.

Search-and-destroy missions were the job of American infantry-men, nicknamed "grunts." Small groups of infantrymen patrolled the sweltering swamps, forests, and jungles of South Vietnam for days at a time, each man "grunting" under the weight of seventy to one hundred pounds of clothes, equipment, and ammunition. As they slogged through the mud and water and hacked their way through the dense undergrowth, the grunts were constantly on edge. Village and jungle trails were often laced with crude but deadly booby traps and land mines. An unseen enemy lurked in the shadows. The guerrillas were patient, hiding out in their own familiar territory and striking only when their forces had a clear advantage. After days of quiet misery, an American patrol might suddenly walk into an ambush—a round of sniper fire or a brief but fierce firefight. When the grunts radioed for air and artillery support, the Vietcong slipped back into the jungle or down an elaborate underground tunnel system that they had dug out for miles into the countryside.

The measure of success in U.S. ground operations was the "body count." Each day combat leaders were required to report the number of enemy soldiers their men had killed. High numbers were used to support the claim that America was winning the war. In reality, many officers wildly exaggerated or even made up their body counts to satisfy their superiors. And in a war against an enemy determined to fight on no matter how great its losses, even high casualty counts had little meaning. Meanwhile, to the soldiers in the field—living in a combat zone with the possibility of death all around, fighting and losing lives over the same ground again and again—the war often seemed like a nightmare with no clear purpose and no end in sight.

## A Grunt Patrols the Jungle

Grunts on search-and-destroy missions were "inserted" into a remote area by helicopter, then left on their own for as long as a week to patrol the countryside. George Olsen was an infantryman in the elite Rangers outfit, specially trained for long-range reconnaissance— searching the jungle for signs of enemy activity. The "abominable terrain" he mentions in this letter to a friend back home included jungles that were so dense the men had to hack their way through step by step. Jungle clearings were dotted with tall bamboo, saw-edged elephant grass, and thorns nearly a foot long. Finding the Vietcong in these natural-camouflage conditions was extremely difficult. The constant strain of watching and listening for hidden enemies wore down even the strongest man. Olsen, who arrived in Vietnam in August 1969, was killed in action in March 1970 at age twenty-three.

15 NOV '69

*Red,*

. . . My team by the day after tomorrow will have gone out 10 times within 40 days, . . . counting the time it takes to get one's equipment in shape—a real accomplishment. The mission before last we set up next to a waterfall in a 360° perimeter, making a hell of a racket

**Charlie/Victor**
*Vietcong*

**Cobra/Huey**
*assault helicopters*

**LZ**
*landing zone*

**POWs**
*prisoners of war*

doing it, I might add. It would appear that the noise of the water killed our noise because when one of our men looked over the boulders we were in, into a hollow next to us, there was Victor in blissful and fatal ignorance that we were less than 20 feet away from him and 15 feet above. We had all the time in the world to get ready, and the surprise was total. After a short and absolutely one-sided fire fight we went through a large base camp which had been hurriedly evacuated, marked it for Cobras, then lit out 800 meters to an LZ with one Victoria Charlie and her three-month-old baby as POWs. We'd just made her a widow, and with all the steel flying in that hollow she was lucky to have escaped unscathed. But I will say that there wasn't a man among us who wasn't glad the child wasn't hit as nobody'd seen either of them during the fight. We'd shoot a female out there without blinking an eye as a woman with a rifle can kill you just as dead as any slant-eyed [fighter]. But a baby is nobody's enemy, and, as I said, it made us all feel better that it hadn't been hurt.

I've just come in from one mission that started out terrible. [We had] to hump three clicks [kilometers] over the most abominable terrain I've ever had the misfortune of encountering. It has become my opinion that the national flower of Vietnam should be an immense thorn. On the second day we heard Victor laughing, talking and raising cain in general, which are sure signs of a nearby base camp—you'd be amazed at the racket Charlie will make when he thinks he's safe in his rear areas. We also heard people in back of us and to our right. We took off for an LZ—you don't go after base camps with seven men and when you're [being] followed unless [you're] sure of surprise. There's no doubt that Charlie knows you're there and is waiting to get enough men to overrun you. With noises getting closer and closer, [I] turned around and waited, hoping Victor would blunder and get close enough to see—no easy accomplishment when visibility is less than 20 feet. I was rear security (last man), and it was a hairy thing listening to people moving all around you and having nothing to fight back at.

*"…maybe it was the noise of my teeth chattering that gave our place away."*

An American adviser leads South Vietnamese army troops into action. To capture this moment on film, a news photographer had to leap from the transport helicopter first, then pause in the open field, exposed to enemy fire.

At one point there was a violent commotion in bushes about 20 feet from me, and I almost cut loose. But then whoever it was took off the other way, so I guess either he saw us without our seeing him, or the lack of movement noises from us tipped him off at the last minute as to what we were doing. I got a few white hairs out of that one, and maybe it was the noise of my teeth chattering that gave our place away, but if I'd ever caught a glimpse of anybody back there, I'd have stitched him from ankle to ears in a heartbeat and been relieved at the prospect. The worst thing in the world is [having] to wait for a rifle bullet to smash into you [before you can] fight back and influence the final outcome of your little duel. We took scattered potshots on the LZ extraction but got out safely with the help of some Cobra gunships. When we extracted, we could hear our friends in back of us yelling and scrambling for cover as the Cobras lined up for their runs. You'll never know how much a man can fall in love with a machine till you've stood on the ground with your head in a noose and had the rope cut at the last minute by a Huey's rotor blades. I'd marry one of those helicopters if it could scratch my back and cook a respectable meal. The day after tomorrow we're going back with

11 men and try for that base camp again, and I sure as hell hope that area has quieted down some or we could definitely wind up in a bind.

*George*

—From Bernard Edelman, editor, Dear America: Letters Home from Vietnam.
New York: W. W. Norton & Company, 1985, 2002.

## THINK ABOUT THIS

1. What difficulties and dangers did Olsen and his team face on their last mission?
2. In another letter to "Red," Olsen reflected on his personal conflicts over how easy it is to kill in wartime. How does this letter hint at his feelings about the necessity and morality of killing?

## Tim O'Brien Walks through a Mine Field

Over one five-year period, booby traps and mines caused 11 percent of the deaths and 17 percent of the injuries among U.S. Army troops in Vietnam. Poorly supplied but ingenious, the Vietcong could make mines out of wood or cardboard, booby traps from nails and bamboo sticks. A cigarette pack or Coke can might contain a deadly explosive; touching a wire or tree along a jungle trail could unleash a bamboo whip tipped with iron spikes or trigger a grenade. Infantry Sergeant Tim O'Brien, who served in Vietnam from 1969 to 1970, describes the paralyzing fear the grunts felt after seeing their buddies maimed or killed by mines.

IT IS NOT EASY TO FIGHT this sort of self-defeating fear, but you try. You decide to be ultracareful—the hard-nosed, realistic approach.

You try to second-guess the mine. Should you put your foot to that flat rock or the clump of weed to its rear? Paddy dike or water? You wish you were Tarzan, able to swing with the vines. You try to trace the footprints of the man to your front. You give it up when he curses you for following too closely; better one man dead than two.

**paddy dike**
*earth embankment around a flooded rice field*

The moment-to-moment, step-by-step decision-making preys on your mind. The effect sometimes is paralysis. You are slow to rise from rest breaks. You walk like a wooden man, like a toy soldier out of Victor Herbert's *Babes in Toyland*. Contrary to military and parental training, you walk with your eyes pinned to the dirt, spine arched, and you are shivering, shoulders hunched. If you are not over-whelmed by complete catatonia, you may react as Philip did on the day he was told to police up one of his friends, victim of an anti-personnel mine. Afterward, as dusk fell, Philip was swinging his entrenching tool like a madman, sweating and crying and hollering. He dug a foxhole four feet into the clay. He sat in it and sobbed. Every-one—all his friends and all the officers—were very quiet, and not a person said anything. No one comforted him until it was very dark. Then, to stop the noise, one man at a time would talk to him, each of us saying he understood and that tomorrow it would all be over. The captain said he would get Philip to the rear, find him a job driving a truck or painting fences.

**police up**
*clean up or clear away*

*"Should you put your foot to that flat rock or the clump of weed to its rear?"*

—*From Tim O'Brien,* If I Die in a Combat Zone. *New York: Delacorte Press, 1973.*

## THINK ABOUT THIS

1. Why do you think O'Brien writes his account mainly in the second person and present tense (*"You decide"*)?

2. What concrete images does he use to help the reader understand what he is experiencing?

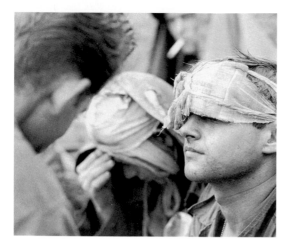

A combat medic treats GIs wounded during the siege of Khe Sanh.

## A Marine Writes from the Trenches of Khe Sanh

While small-scale skirmishes were the rule in the Vietnam War, the North Vietnamese Army occasionally launched major assaults to try to weaken and dishearten American forces. The attack on Khe Sanh was such an assault. Khe Sanh is a small plateau in northwestern South Vietnam that was the site of a U.S. military base. Six thousand marines manned the base on January 21, 1968, when an estimated 20,000 to 40,000 NVA began their attack. For the next seventy-eight days, the Americans lived with hunger, thirst, filth, giant rats and other vermin, and constant smoke and fumes. They held off the attackers through artillery fire and fierce hand-to-hand fighting, while U.S. planes dropped enough explosives and napalm (jellied gasoline dropped in bombs to cover an area with fire) to make Khe Sanh the most heavily bombed area in history. More than 200 marines and perhaps 10,000 to 15,000 NVA were killed before the siege ended on April 7. In this letter to his wife, marine medic David Steinberg describes the conditions in the trenches on one of the hill outposts of Khe Sanh.

JANUARY 29, 1968

*My Dearest Sharon,*

This is your favorite caveman in the beautiful resort area on Hill 881S. There are great accommodations if you pick-and-shovel out a little hole to sleep in. The surrounding countryside is in full bloom, with assorted bomb craters and napalm-burnt hills to add to the beauty. Sunbathing while filling sandbags increases one's muscles while at the same time it tends to keep the waistline trim. C-rations are passed out three times a day, and a quarter-canteen per day keeps one's water intake to a minimum. Whenever a helicopter stops in with troops or supplies, the NVA give them a hearty welcome with three or four mortars or rockets. We in turn join the festival by shooting 2,000 rounds into the beautiful countryside from our automatic weapons. Hot during the day, freezing at night, with a fireworks display nightly all add to the great vacationing fun on the mountain called 881S.

**C-rations**
*combat rations*

Well, dear, I'm still hanging in here despite the fun. I'm about due for R&R, but I'll wait until next month. I think I'll go to Taipei.

**R & R**
*"rest and relaxation"; a short leave*

Well, Sharon dear, I best get some sleep and maybe dream of you again. Don't worry or be mad if the letters don't come as often, because I don't even know if mail is leaving this damn hill.

I miss you very much and my love is mounting and my impatience to be with you again is slowly coming to a boil. I'm determined to make it home, and even if I have to spend my next two months in a whole mess of mud and trenches, ole Charlie won't keep me.

Gotta cut now and heat up a Meal, Combat, Individual, Beef, Spiced with Sauce, Cookies, Cocoa, White Bread, Canned. Love them C-rations! An assortment of twelve to choose from for a whole year.

—*From Eric Hammel,* Khe Sanh: Siege in the Clouds. *New York: Crown, 1989.*

## THINK ABOUT THIS

1. Soldiers in wartime often use humor to relieve the tensions of combat. What humorous or ironic words and images does Steinberg use in his letter?

2. Reading "between the lines," what can you tell about the true picture of conditions during the siege of Khe Sanh?

# A Veteran-Poet Reflects on "Guerrilla War"

William Ehrhart joined the marines at age seventeen and served in Vietnam from 1967 to 1968. In an interview for a television documentary, he described the frustration GIs felt simply trying to identify the enemy.

AND SO, DAY AFTER DAY, you had dead Marines, wounded Marines, and nobody to fight back at. In the meantime, . . . you're on a patrol, somebody hits a mine and there's a couple of dead people. And here's Joe the rice farmer out in his field. He just, he don't even stop. He don't even, it's like he didn't even hear the blast. And after awhile, you start thinking, wait, these people must know where these mines are. How come they never step on them? They must be VC [Vietcong]. They must be VC sympathizers. And so, over a relatively short period of time, you begin to treat all Vietnamese as though they are the enemy.

> *"...you begin to treat all Vietnamese as though they are the enemy."*

—*From* Vietnam: A Television History, *"Episode 5: America Takes Charge, 1965–1967."*

After the war's end Ehrhart became one of the most well-known Vietnam veteran-poets. In "Guerrilla War," he uses poetry to present ideas similar to those expressed above.

It's practically impossible
to tell civilians
from the Vietcong.

Nobody wears uniforms.
They all talk
the same language
(and you couldn't understand them
even if they didn't).

They tape grenades
inside their clothes,
and carry satchel charges
in their market baskets.

Even their women fight;
and young boys,
and girls.

It's practically impossible
to tell civilians from the Vietcong;

after awhile,
you quit trying.

—From W. D. Ehrhart, Beautiful Wreckage: New & Selected Poems by
W. D. Ehrhart. *Easthampton, MA: Adastra Press, 1999.*

## THINK ABOUT THIS

1. Who do you think is "speaking" in Ehrhart's poem, and who is that person's audience?

2. How does the experience of reading Ehrhart's poem differ from that of reading his spoken narrative? Is one clearer than the other? Easier to understand? More emotionally expressive?

# Chapter 3

# The War at Home: "Doves" for Peace

I N THE EARLY YEARS OF the Vietnam War, the great majority of Americans supported their government's stand against communism. After 1965, though, when President Lyndon Johnson sent in the first combat troops, voices of doubt and dissent were raised and quickly swelled to a chorus of protests. In April 1967 more than 200,000 Americans descended on New York City and San Francisco in massive antiwar rallies. In October another 50,000 marched in Washington, D.C. By early 1968 the mounting protests—heightened by outrage over the Tet Offensive—had forced President Johnson to withdraw from his reelection campaign. Two years later, President Richard Nixon's widening of the war with strikes against Vietnam's neighbor Cambodia sent antiwar protests to a new height. There were huge demonstrations on college campuses, many marked by violence. Until the end of the war, the protests would continue across the country, including one march on Washington in April 1971 that drew some 750,000 protesters—the largest antiwar rally in U.S. history.

An antiwar rally in Washington, D.C. American involvement
in Vietnam divided the nation into two hostile camps—
antiwar "doves" versus prowar "hawks."

At first the "doves"—those who opposed the Vietnam War—included mainly pacifists (people who oppose all violence), religious leaders, social activists, and college students. Young people had a special interest in the war—it was their generation doing the fighting and dying. As the fighting intensified and casualties rose, the opposition became more widespread. Members of Congress and other political leaders, artists and entertainers, doctors and scientists, businessmen and homemakers, and even a growing number of Vietnam veterans joined the antiwar movement. In October 1967 polls showed that for the first time a majority of Americans believed that sending troops to Vietnam had been a mistake. While most of these people never joined an antiwar group or took part in a demonstration, many did. It was no longer surprising to see teachers marching in protest beside their students, parents beside their children.

Antiwar protests took many forms. Most were peaceful: petitions and letter writing, "teach-ins" during which college students and professors spoke out against the war, sit-ins and picket lines at military recruiting centers or war-supply manufacturers, marches and rallies. As time went on and frustrations grew, some protesters turned to more radical tactics. They burned their draft cards or the American flag, seized college buildings, blocked troop trains carrying Vietnam-bound GIs, and broke into draft offices and destroyed the records. In October 1967 demonstrators stormed the Pentagon, and military police struck back with tear gas and nightsticks. There were other demonstrations that also ended in bloody confrontations with police or National Guardsmen, with many protesters arrested or beaten and a few killed.

The question of whether the antiwar movement helped end the Vietnam War is still a subject of debate. Some people argue that the protests only encouraged the enemy and so actually prolonged the war. Others maintain that antiwar actions kept the spotlight on government policy, persuading Congress and the American public that the war was a mistake and finally forcing the government to stop escalating and make peace.

## A Bitter Soldier Asks "Why?"

No one had earned a better right to pass judgment on American policy in Vietnam than the soldiers sent to serve there. In the early years of the war, many young men went to Vietnam with a mission to fight the spread of communism. Over time, many found their sense of purpose clouded by suspicions that the war was being poorly run, that the costs were too high, that perhaps Americans shouldn't be fighting at all. At the same time, many GIs felt betrayed by the people back home, who seemed indifferent or even hostile to their service and sacrifices. Infantry sergeant Phillip Woodall voices these frustrations and doubts in a letter to his father, written a day after the Reverend Martin Luther King's assassination in Memphis, Tennessee.

APRIL 5 '68
LZ Sally
*Dear Dad—*
. . . On Friday, March 29, in our AO just south of Hue near the ocean, we received small-arms fire from a village. Two platoons went into the

**AO**
*area of operations*

village. Our platoon maneuvered to the right, attempting to set up a blocking force so when the NVA were pushed out of the village we could cut them off. My job was carrying the platoon radio. My platoon leader, Gary Scott, 2nd lieutenant, Infantry, was in command. Lt. Scott, a Negro from Rochester, New York, graduated recently from the University of Syracuse.

As the platoon moved toward the rear of the village, automatic-weapons fire suddenly came from a near woodline. Lt. Scott and one other man were killed, another seriously wounded. I was very close to Lt. Scott. I was his radio operator. He was a fine man, a good leader, yet he could not understand the whys of this conflict which called him 10,000 miles from his home, to a land of insects, poverty and hostility—this conflict which killed him. Why?

> *"We're fighting, dying, for a people who resent our being over here."*

Fighting for a people who have no concern for the war, people he did not understand, [who] knew where the enemy were, where the booby traps were hidden yet gave no support. People that he would give portions of his food to yet would try to sell him a Coke for $1.00. People who cared not who the winner was—yet they will say he died for his country, keeping it free. Negative. [Vietnam] is no gain that I can see, Dad. We're fighting, dying, for a people who resent our being over here. The only firm reason I can find is paying with commie lives for U.S. lives, Dad.

Tonight the nation mourns the death of Martin Luther King. Not me. I mourn the deaths of the real leaders for peace, the people who give the real sacrifice, people like Lt. Scott. Tonight as the nation mourns Dr. King, they drink their cold beer, turn on their air conditioner and watch their TV. We who mourn the deaths over here will set up our ambushes, pull our guard and eat our C-rations.

I will probably get a Bronze Star for the fire fight. Lt. Scott will get a Silver Star. That will help me get a job someday and it is supposed to suffice for Lt. Scott's life. I guess I'm bitter now, Dad. This war is all wrong. I will continue to fight, win my medals and fight the elements and hardships of this country. But that is because I'm a soldier and it's my job and there are other people depending on me. That's my excuse. That's all I have, theories and excuses—no solutions.

Your loving son,
*Phil*

—*From Bernard Edelman, editor,* Dear America: Letters Home from Vietnam.
*New York: W. W. Norton & Company, 1985, 2002.*

## THINK ABOUT THIS

1. What points does Woodall make to support his conclusion that the Vietnam War is "all wrong"?
2. What are his reasons for continuing to serve in spite of his negative feelings about the war?

# An Antiwar Petition Opposes the "Crime of Silence"

Among the many peaceful forms of protest used by antiwar activists were petitions. These were usually circulated on college campuses and city streets to gather as many signatures as possible, then sent to government decision makers. Hundreds of thousands of people signed this antiwar declaration and mailed it to the secretary general of the United Nations to voice their opposition to the Vietnam War.

# Individuals Against the Crime of Silence

**A Declaration** **To Our Fellow Citizens Of The United States, To The Peoples Of The World, And To Future Generations:**

**1** We are appalled and angered by the conduct of our country in Vietnam.

**2** In the name of liberty, we have unleashed the awesome arsenal of the greatest military power in the world upon a small agricultural nation, killing, burning and mutilating its people. In the name of peace, we are creating a desert. In the name of security, we are inviting world conflagration.

**3** We, the signers of this declaration, believe this war to be immoral. We believe it to be illegal. We must oppose it.

**4** At Nuremberg, after World War II, we tried, convicted and executed men for the crime of OBEYING their government, when that government demanded of them crimes against humanity. Millions more, who were not tried, were still guilty of THE CRIME OF SILENCE.

**5** We have a commitment to the laws and principles we carefully forged in the AMERICAN CONSTITUTION, at the NUREMBERG TRIALS, and in the UNITED NATIONS CHARTER. And our own deep democratic traditions and our dedication to the ideal of human decency among men demand that we speak out.

**We Therefore** **wish to declare our names to the office of the Secretary General of the United Nations, both as permanent witness to our opposition to the war in Vietnam and as a demonstration that the conscience of America is not dead.**

On September 23, 1965, a Memorandum of Law was incorporated in the Congressional Record of the 89th Congress of the United States of America, in which leading American attorneys, after careful analysis of our position and actions in the Vietnam War, came to the conclusion that the U.S. is violating the following accords: The Charter of the United Nations, The Geneva Accords of 1954, the United States Constitution.

**To Protest — To Object — To Dissent** has long been an American tradition. The following are a few among the many who have signed this declaration to be on permanent record.

| | | | |
|---|---|---|---|
| ABE AJAY | NAOMI L. GOLDSTEIN | HERBERT D. MAGIDSON | ROBERT RYAN |
| JAMES BALDWIN | DR. RALPH R. GREENSON | SHIRLEY MAGIDSON | DAVID SCHOENBRUN |
| (FATHER) J. E. BAMBERGER, M.D. OCSO | PROF. ABRAHAM J. HESCHEL | NORMAN MAILER | LORRY SHERMAN |
| DANIEL BERRIGAN, S.J. | BRIG. GENERAL H. B. HESTER, RET. | THOMAS MERTON | PROF. ROBERT SIMMONS |
| REV. PHILLIP BERRIGAN, S.S.J. | DR. STANLEY HOFFMAN | SIDNEY MEYER | DR. BENJAMIN SPOCK |
| RAY BRADBURY | CHARLES H. HUBBEL | EASON MONROE | FRED H. STEINMETZ, ESQ. |
| ROBERT McAFFEE BROWN | PROF. DONALD KALISH | PROF. HANS J. MORGENTHAU | DR. NORMAN TABACHNICK |
| REV. WILLIAM H. DU BAY | EDWARD M. KEATING | HENRY E. NILES | D. IAN THIERMANN |
| JAMES FARMER | PHIL KERBY | DR. MARK F. ORFIRER | BRYNA IVENS UNTERMEYER |
| W. H. FERRY | PAULINE KRAMER | AVA HELEN PAULING | LOUIS UNTERMEYER |
| ROSE S. FIELDS | RING LARDNER, JR. | DR. LINUS PAULING | DICK VAN DYKE |
| DR. JEROME D. FRANK | RABBI RICHARD N. LEVY | BISHOP JAMES A. PIKE | ROBERT VAUGHN |
| REV. STEPHEN H. FRITCHMAN | LOUIS LICHT, ESQ. | RICHARD M. POWELL | DR. MAURICE N. WALSH |
| BEN GAZZARA | DR. ROBERT E. LITMAN | CARL REINER | DR. HARVEY WHEELER |
| DR. FRED GOLDSTEIN | VICTOR LUDWIG | JANICE RULE | A. L. WIRIN, ESQ. |

—From "Individuals against the Crime of Silence" antiwar petition, 1969.

1. The petition compares people who do not speak out against the Vietnam War to those who remained silent during the Nazi atrocities of World War II. Do you think this is a fair and reasonable comparison?

2. Why do you think the petition writers included the names of famous doctors, scientists, writers, actors, and other celebrities at the bottom of the document? Would a list like this influence your decision to sign a petition?

3. What role has dissent played in American history?

# A Reporter Runs with Rioters in Chicago

While most antiwar protests were peaceful, some turned ugly. Chicago was the scene of two of the worst episodes. The first came in August 1968, during the Democratic National Convention. As delegates met in the convention hall to choose the Democratic Party's candidate for president, five thousand demonstrators clashed with police and National Guardsmen outside. The violent free-for-all wounded hundreds of people, including both protesters and innocent bystanders. About a year later, the city exploded again. A radical group called the Weathermen scheduled "Four Days of Rage" in Chicago, hoping to provoke a crisis that would lead to a full-scale "mass revolutionary movement" against American government and society. Although the group predicted that "10,000 revolutionaries" would join them, only about 300 showed up. On the night of October 8, 1969, *Chicago Sun-Times* reporter Tom Fitzpatrick ran with the rioters to find out who they were and what made them fight.

BAD MARVIN HAD BEEN STANDING in front of the fire he had made of a Lincoln Park bench for about 30 minutes, shouting to everyone in the crowd and warning them how bad he was.

It was 10:25 P.M. . . . and now about 200 kids began racing out of the park, heading toward the Chicago Historical Society. Bad Marvin started running, too, brandishing a long piece of burning board in his right hand.

"Viva Ché," he kept shouting as he ran. "Viva Cuba."

"Bring the war home now," screamed a girl running alongside him.

She was so caught up with running in the dark that she ran right into a large tree outside the Historical Society and collapsed in a lump, the first casualty of the night.

By now the main force of the group had reached North Federal Savings, at the northwest corner of North and Clark. It's a big, impressive building with large plate glass windows and here's where the tide turned.

A tall skinny kid in a white helmet ran a little in front of the crowd and tossed a rock through one of the large windows. The first rock was soon followed by a second and a third, and then cheering. . . .

The sound of shattering glass hits everyone in the group like an electric shock. You are not alone when you are in a group like this. From now on, it was going to have to be a wild ride. And if you were going to find out what happened, you had to go along with it.

By this time you have already learned one important rule about running with mobs who are tossing rocks. You have to stay up front and stay right on the street with them.

If you get on the sidewalk, you'll never see the rock that hits you instead of an apartment window. There is a risk in this, too, because you must time your moves so that you get away from the whole outfit as soon as you see the line of police forming ahead of you.

The police weren't in sight and the wild march went on all the

**Ché**
*Cuban revolutionary leader Ché Guevara*

way to within 50 yards of Division Street. And there the police were waiting.

They were lined up across the street and they weren't saying a word. It was a sight so formidable that you didn't blame the kids when they turned and ran back north on Clark and then turned east on Goethe to escape.

Goethe was where it really got bad. Every car window for a two-block stretch was smashed and so were the lobby windows of a high-rise apartment on the corner of Dearborn and Goethe.

The kids knew it was all over for them but they kept on the attack.

And now, as we're heading into the eye of the storm on Division Street, I see a beautiful thing happen. It's Bad Marvin, the guy with the flaming stock who was bragging to everyone how bad he was going to be. Bad Marvin is running away and his torch has burned out.

**stock**
*block of wood*

It always makes you feel good when the tough-talking guys cave in, but now what does happen is not good. All the kids who have been wound up so tight from listening to the inflammatory speeches in the park are going to take it in the head.

"Charge!" one little kid screams as he runs for the police line. "Charge!" the cry comes back as about a dozen more follow him.

The squad cars are at the intersection and the kids are being thrown into them as quickly as possible. One policeman is leaning over a squad car holding his head. He's been hit by a rock and he's bleeding and he's mad. . . .

You can see at least three of them have their revolvers drawn. The others are wielding clubs.

The kids run but they don't have a chance. They have been asking all night for a confrontation and now they get one.

*"The sound of shattering glass hits everyone in the group like an electric shock."*

Within minutes the street is cleared and Deputy Supt. James Rochford is walking toward Sgt. James Clark to get a final report. But there is no smile of triumph on Rochford's face. He was through this

A delegate to the 1968 Democratic National Convention protests a policy vote by trying to set fire to his plastic ID card. The many helping hands and smiling faces indicate that this was a friendly disagreement, in sharp contrast to the violent clashes taking place in the streets outside the convention hall.

same thing during the Democratic National Convention of 1968 and he didn't take any delight in it then, either.

"All right," Rochford says to Clark. "Get the men to clear the street. Let's all just get out of here."

—From Tom Fitzpatrick, "A Wild Night's Ride in Chicago," Chicago Sun-Times, October 9, 1969; reprinted in John Hohenberg, editor, The Pulitzer Prize Story II, 1959–1980. New York: Columbia University Press, 1980.

## THINK ABOUT THIS

1. Fitzpatrick won a Pulitzer Prize for this account, which the awards board called "an excellent job of objective reporting and good writing." What are some examples of the report's objectivity?

2. While Fitzpatrick's main goal is to describe the experience of running with the rioters, he also provides clues about the feelings of the police who confront them. How would you describe the attitude of the police?

## The *Akron Beacon Journal* Covers a Tragedy at Kent State

After President Nixon announced on April 30, 1970, that he was sending U.S. troops into Cambodia, demonstrations broke out at hundreds of college campuses. At Kent State University in Ohio, students rioted and set fire to the ROTC (Reserve Officers' Training Corps) building on campus. National Guardsmen were called in to restore order. During a rally on May 4, held to protest the guard's presence, a few students began throwing rocks. A group of guardsmen opened fire, killing four students. A team of reporters and photographers from the *Akron Beacon Journal,* on the scene to cover the disturbances, put together the following report, which was published that afternoon.

KENT—Four persons were killed and at least 11 others shot as National Guardsmen fired into a group of rock-throwing protesters at Kent State university today.

Three of the dead were tentatively identified as William Schroeder, Jeffrey Miller, and Allison Krause. The fourth was an unidentified girl [Sandra Scheuer]. . . .

Gunshots rang out about 12:30 P.M., half an hour after Guardsmen fired tear gas into a crowd of 500 on the Commons behind the university administration offices. Demonstrators hurled rocks and tear gas grenades back as they scattered. . . .

A newspaperman, an eyewitness to the shooting, said the gunshots were fired after one student hurled a rock as Guardsmen were turning away after clearing the Commons.

"One section of the Guard turned around and fired and then all the Guardsmen turned and fired," he said.

*Clockwise from top left:* William Schroeder, Allison Krause, Jeffrey Miller, Sandra Scheuer. These four students were killed during a confrontation between anti-war protesters and National Guardsmen at Kent State University in May 1970.

According to the witness, some of the Guardsmen were firing in the air while others were firing straight ahead. . . .

The shooting broke out after students had rallied on the Commons in defiance of an order not to assemble.

An officer in a jeep ordered them over a loud speaker to disperse. He begged them to break up "for your own good." The protesters laughed and jeered. The troops, wearing gas masks, then began to launch canisters of tear gas.

The troops were en route back to their original positions when about 20 students, both boys and girls, ran toward them from behind Taylor Hall.

Stones and sticks fell on the troops and obscenities filled the air.

Apparently without orders, the Guardsmen turned and aimed their M-1 rifles at the charging students and began firing.

Students in the emergency ward at Robinson Memorial Hospital said they wanted to get on the Commons to discuss demands.

> *"Apparently without orders, the Guardsmen turned and aimed their M-1 rifles."*

They said that as they started gathering the Guardsmen began throwing "pepper" gas at them and the students started throwing rocks.

Then, they said, the firing started. . . .

Militants in three nights have burned the University's ROTC Building, smashed 56 downtown store windows and threatened Kent businessmen. . . .

The rioting Friday night came a day after President Nixon told the nation he was sending troops into Cambodia.

—From "All the Guardsmen Turned and Fired," Akron Beacon Journal, *May 4, 1970*.

## THINK ABOUT THIS

1. How does this report answer the five basic questions of good journalism: who, what, when, where, and how?

2. Would you say that this is a balanced report? Why or why not?

# Chapter 4

# The War at Home: "Hawks" for War

NOT ALL AMERICANS JOINED the antiwar movement. Many continued to support the government's policy in Vietnam. These "hawks" included men and women of all ages, from all walks of life. The majority were conservative members of the older generation, including hundreds of thousands of working-class Americans: mechanics, carpenters, seamen, bricklayers, autoworkers, construction workers. Hawks considered doves unpatriotic. They believed that the students and intellectuals who opposed the war were overprivileged brats attacking a country that had given them everything. Disturbed by the conflicts and changes disrupting society, they longed for a return to "normalcy" and law and order. In their anger the hawks lashed out at the "longhairs" who seemed to be challenging not just the war but also traditional American values and the American way of life.

In May 1967, 70,000 hawks marched in New York City, carrying American flags and banners with slogans reading "Down with the Reds," "Support Our Boys," and "America—Love It or Leave It." A May 1970 rally attracted nearly 100,000 war supporters. Hawks not only held

Construction workers rally in New York City in support of the Vietnam war
effort. Like the flags they carry, the hard hats many of them are wearing
had become a symbol of patriotism to working-class Americans.

their own rallies and marches but sometimes disrupted antiwar demonstrations. During at least one peace rally in New York in 1970, construction workers assaulted the protesters while city police stood watching.

Despite their hatred of the antiwar forces, many hawks gradually came to share their point of view. Particularly after the Tet Offensive in 1968, the ranks of war supporters dwindled and many former hawks began calling for withdrawal from Vietnam. Their reasons were personal and practical. Far more sons of working-class Americans were fighting in Vietnam than boys from wealthy upper-class families, who usually found ways to avoid the draft. Also, as the war dragged on, even some of the most die-hard hawks became convinced that it was a mistake—that the American strategy was not working and that the cost in dollars and lives was too high. Some blamed the antiwar movement itself for the deteriorating situation in Vietnam. Protesters had caused so much trouble, these critics claimed, that they had forced Americans to fight with one hand tied behind their back, ensuring defeat.

Even when hawks and doves agreed the war should end, they remained bitter enemies. One working-class man who had changed from a pro- to an antiwar stance expressed the often contradictory emotions felt by many Americans during the Vietnam War: "It's people like us who give our sons for the country. I hate those peace demonstrators. . . . The sooner we get the hell out of [Vietnam] the better."

## President Johnson Explains Why America Is in Vietnam

Lyndon Johnson inherited the war in Vietnam along with the presidency after John F. Kennedy's assassination in 1963. The new president had little experience in foreign affairs. His main area of interest was domestic policy, especially the Great Society programs he introduced to fight poverty and protect civil rights at home. But Johnson was also a strong anti-Communist who vowed, "I am not going to be the president who saw Southeast Asia go the way China went." At first, he proceeded cautiously in Vietnam, expanding the program of military advisers and economic aid that had been begun by earlier presidents. But gradually, as it became clear that these programs were not working, Johnson expanded the war through the increasing use of direct U.S. military action against North Vietnam. In April 1965, a month after he began the Rolling Thunder bombing campaign and sent in the first combat troops, President Johnson spoke at Johns Hopkins University in Baltimore, Maryland. This address was one of his first major speeches defending U.S. involvement in Vietnam.

WHY ARE WE IN South Viet-Nam?

*We are there because we have a promise to keep.* Since 1954 every American President has offered support to the people of South Viet-Nam. We have helped to build, and we have helped to defend. Thus, over many years, we have made a national pledge to help South Viet-Nam defend its independence.

And I intend to keep that promise. . . .

*We are also there to strengthen world order.* Around the globe, from Berlin to Thailand, are people whose well-being rests, in part, on the belief that they can count on us if they are attacked. To leave Viet-Nam to its fate would shake the confidence of all these people in the value of an American commitment and in the value of America's word. The result would be increased unrest and instability, and even wider war.

A GI points to a bullet hole in his helmet that fortunately only caused a headache. President Johnson struggled hard over his decision to send the first American combat troops to Vietnam.

*We are also there because there are great stakes in the balance.* Let no one think for a moment that retreat from Viet-Nam would bring an end to conflict. The battle would be renewed in one country and then another. The central lesson of our time is that the appetite of aggression is never satisfied. To withdraw from one battlefield means only to prepare for the next. We must say in southeast Asia—as we did in Europe [in World War II]—in the words of the Bible: "Hitherto shalt thou come, but no further." . . .

Our objective is the independence of South Viet-Nam, and its freedom from attack. We want nothing for ourselves—only that the people of South Viet-Nam be allowed to guide their own country in their own way.

We will do everything necessary to reach that objective. And we will do only what is absolutely necessary.

—*From* Public Papers of the Presidents of the United States: Lyndon B. Johnson, 1965. *Washington, D.C.: U.S. Government Printing Office, 1967.*

## THINK ABOUT THIS

**1.** What reasons does Johnson give for U.S. involvement in Vietnam? Do you find his arguments convincing? Why or why not?

2. Who, in addition to the American public, is the intended audience for Johnson's speech? What points might be intended for a wider audience?

3. In your opinion, to what extent does the United States have a duty to help maintain world order?

# A GI Explains the War to American Schoolchildren

Many American soldiers, especially in the early stages of the war, went to Vietnam proud to serve their country and fight the evils of communism. In their view it was better to combat communism in South Vietnam than to wait until it spread to Hawaii or California or their own backyard. Private First Class (later Sergeant) Robert Jackman was a truck driver with the U.S. Army Headquarters Area Command in Saigon. After he received a letter from an American elementary school class, Jackman sent this reply, explaining why he and other soldiers believed it was important to make a stand in Vietnam.

21 MAY 66

*Dear Class C-4,*

South Vietnam is a very small country struggling to keep its freedom. Many of the little boys and girls in South Vietnam may never have the opportunities that you children will have. Nevertheless, the children of South Vietnam are very much like yourselves in the games they play and the things they do. I am enclosing some paper toys that the boys and girls of Vietnam play with. I hope that you enjoy the toys as much as they do. In Vietnam, the little things mean a lot more than the big things.

It is nice to know that you children are safe and sound in America. The reason that I and all the other soldiers are in Vietnam is so that you children will always be safe in our great country. Thank you all again for thinking of me in this strange land. I hope that all the soldiers in Vietnam have as many boys and girls thinking about [them] as I do.

Sincerely yours,
*PFC Robert B. Jackman*

*—From Bernard Edelman, editor,* Dear America: Letters Home from Vietnam. *New York: W. W. Norton & Company, 1985, 2002.*

## THINK ABOUT THIS

1. How does Jackman make his arguments clear and convincing to young children?
2. How do you think he might have rephrased his letter to explain his position to an older audience?

## President Nixon Appeals to the "Silent Majority"

During the 1968 presidential campaign, Republican candidate Richard Nixon claimed that he had a "secret plan" to "end the war and win the peace" in Vietnam. In reality, there was no plan. Once he took office in January 1969, Nixon found himself facing the same predicament as former President Johnson had—how to bring the war to an end without seeming to abandon an ally and cave in to the Communists. The strategy Nixon chose was Vietnamization, the gradual withdrawal of U.S. combat troops accompanied by increased air attacks on the North and massive shipments of arms and aid to South Vietnam. In this televised speech to the nation on November 3, 1969, Nixon explains the policy of Vietnamization and appeals for support from the "great silent majority" of Americans who have been "turned off" by the excesses of the antiwar movement.

*"A nation cannot remain great if it betrays its allies and lets down its friends."*

THE QUESTION FACING US TODAY IS: Now that we are in the war, what is the best way to end it?

In January I could only conclude that the precipitate [too fast] withdrawal of American forces from Vietnam would be a disaster not only for South Vietnam but for the United States and for the cause of peace.

For the South Vietnamese, our precipitate withdrawal would inevitably allow the Communists to repeat the massacres which followed their takeover in the North 15 years before. . . .

For the United States, this first defeat in our Nation's history would result in a collapse of confidence in American leadership, not only in Asia but throughout the world. . . .

A nation cannot remain great if it betrays its allies and lets down its friends.

Our defeat and humiliation in South Vietnam without question would promote recklessness in the councils of those great powers who have not yet abandoned their goals of world conquest.

This would spark violence wherever our commitments help maintain the peace—in the Middle East, in Berlin, eventually even in the Western Hemisphere.

Ultimately, this would cost more lives.

It would not bring peace; it would bring more war. . . .

My fellow Americans, I am sure you recognize from what I have said that we really only have two choices open to us if we want to end this war.

I can order an immediate, precipitate withdrawal of all Americans from Vietnam without regard to the effects of that action.

Or we can persist in our search for a just peace through a negotiated settlement if possible, or through continued implementation of our plan for Vietnamization if necessary—a plan in which we will withdraw all our forces from Vietnam on a schedule in accordance with our program, as the South Vietnamese become strong enough to defend their own freedom.

I have chosen this second course.

It is not the easy way.

It is the right way. . . .

I recognize that some of my fellow citizens disagree with the plan for peace I have chosen. Honest and patriotic Americans have reached different conclusions as to how peace should be achieved.

In San Francisco a few weeks ago, I saw demonstrators carrying signs reading "Lose in Vietnam, bring our boys home."

Well, one of the strengths of our free society is that any American has a right to reach that conclusion and to advocate that point of view. But as President of the United States, I would be untrue to my oath of office if I allowed the policy of this Nation to be dictated by the minority who hold that point of view and who try to impose it on the Nation by mounting demonstrations in the street. . . .

And so tonight—to you, the great silent majority of my fellow Americans—I ask for your support.

I pledged in my campaign for the Presidency to end the war in a way that we could win the peace. I have initiated a plan of action which will enable me to keep that pledge.

The more support I can have from the American people, the sooner that pledge can be redeemed; for the more divided we are at home, the less likely the enemy is to negotiate at Paris.

Let us be united for peace. Let us also be united against defeat.

Because let us understand: North Vietnam cannot defeat or humiliate the United States. Only Americans can do that.

—*From* Public Papers of the Presidents of the United States: Richard M. Nixon, 1969. *Washington, D.C.: U.S. Government Printing Office, 1971.*

## THINK ABOUT THIS

1. What reasons does President Nixon give for U.S. involvement in Vietnam? How are these similar to or different from the reasons given by President Johnson in his April 1965 speech (see page 41)?

2. According to conversations between Nixon and his aides, one of the president's goals in making this speech was to put critics of his policies "on the run" and to encourage hawks to unite against the antiwar movement. What arguments does he use to accomplish those goals? Are his arguments based on reason or emotion?

# A Member of the "Silent Majority" Speaks

One of the battlegrounds in the war between hawks and doves was the pages of local newspapers. Thousands of Americans on both sides of the conflict argued their case in the "Letters to the Editor" columns of their hometown papers. In May 1969 John Cartinhour of Livingston, New Jersey, wrote to express a view shared by some of the angriest members of President Nixon's "silent majority": that the antiwar protesters were traitors to their country, just as dangerous as the Communists America was fighting in Vietnam.

DEAR SIR:

I have been reading with interest the stories in the papers about the antics of left-wing students around the country. The whole situation—

demonstrations, riots, and what have you—has become intolerable. In the case of certain college students—bearded leftist brats who demonstrate and riot against America while living off the old man's hard-earned money—there is only one solution: kick them out of college. They have no "right" to be there, as they seem to think. In the case of high school leftists who cause trouble, I suggest that in addition to enforcing the rules of law and order in school, the school authorities refuse to recommend any of these brats for admission to a college.

These leftists mean business every step of the way. Obviously their goal is to destroy the United States of America. This is why patriotic Americans have got to act now to put a stop to all this trouble. You see, we are not only fighting the Communists in Vietnam. We are fighting them within the United States itself.

As for the war in Vietnam, I have read in your paper several letters from Livingston High School students who belong to, or support, an outfit called "Students for Peace." These students point out, correctly, that over 10,000 American soldiers have been killed in Vietnam since the "peace talks" started. According to these students, this is an intolerable state of events.

This hippie couple's long hair and casual clothes look perfectly natural today. To millions of clean-cut, conservative older Americans in the 1960s and 1970s, however, the younger generation's lifestyle was a bewildering assault on traditional American values.

They are quite right. But they had better get one thing straight right now: the only way to bring peace to Vietnam is to WIN the war, win it quickly, and win it decisively. Appeasement of Communism will bring "peace," all right; the peace of the slave, though, as compared to the peace of the strong and free.

One thing is for sure, and people who sincerely want peace had better realize it soon: There can be no peace until the international Communist conspiracy is defeated and destroyed.

*"...patriotic Americans have got to act now."*

One final comment: It is easy to spot the phoney advocates of peace in Vietnam. They are the ones who see little wrong with the Communist side of the war, but see everything wrong with what the United States does. These people are not for peace. They are traitors in every moral sense of the word. The only "peace" they long for is that of an enslaved America.

Sincerely,
*John Cartinhour, Jr.*

—*From the Livingston, New Jersey,* West Essex Tribune, *May 22, 1969.*

## THINK ABOUT THIS

1. How do you think Cartinhour would define "patriotism"?
2. In his view, how should school authorities respond to students who demonstrate against the war? Are his suggestions legal?

## Servicemen React to Protests at Home

Many of the servicemen in Vietnam were enraged by the antiwar movement. Often, even those who had begun to question American policy felt that antiwar protests insulted the men who were serving their country and those who had given their lives in that service. Gregory Lusco served in Vietnam from 1968 to 1970 with the army's 101st Airborne Division. On July 23, 1970, the *Greenfield* (Massachusetts) *Recorder* published this angry letter written by Lusco and nineteen fellow soldiers.

[DEAR EDITOR:]

. . . This letter is from the men who daily risk their lives in the air over the war-wrought land of Vietnam. It is the combined thoughts and beliefs of 1st and 2nd flight platoons, B Company, 159th Aviation Battalion, 101st Airborne Division, and you can believe me that a lot of our descriptive phrases are being omitted due to the grossness and obscenities of them.

*"... you have forced and caused these men to die for nothing."*

The outburst of raw violence and malice spontaneously occurred when the following quotation was read aloud to them from a letter: "We've had some memorial services for them at school and there's a movement for a strike." The quotation was in regards to the recent killings at Kent in Ohio. We are sorrowful and mourn the dead, but it grieves us no end and shoots pain into our hearts that the "biggest upset is over the kids who got killed at Kent."

So why don't your hearts cry out and shed a tear for the 40-plus thousand red-blooded Americans and brave, fearless, loyal men who have given their lives so a bunch of . . . radicals can protest, dissent and generally bitch about our private and personal war in Vietnam and now Cambodia?

During my past 18 months in hell I've seen and held my friends during their last gasping seconds before they succumbed to death. And not once . . . did they chastise our country's involvement in Vietnam. . . .

Last month my company lost 12 good men and five more were torn up so bad that they have been sent back to the States. We shed true tears for these men. What did you do? Protest. In your feeble and deteriorating and filthy degenerate minds you have forced and caused these men to die for nothing. Do you place such a low value on our heads? We are trying to end the war so that our loved ones will never have to face the harsh realities of death in our own country.

Do not judge us wrongly. We are not pleading for your praise. All we ask is for our great nation to unite and stand behind President Nixon. Support us, help us end the war, . . . save our lives. . . .

With love,

*Greg Lusco*

PHU BAI, SOUTH VIETNAM

—*From Bernard Edelman, editor,* Dear America: Letters Home from Vietnam. *New York: W. W. Norton & Company, 1985, 2002.*

## THINK ABOUT THIS

1. What feelings prompted Lusco and his fellow soldiers to write their letter? Why do you think they sent it to Lusco's hometown newspaper?
2. Why do the writers feel that antiwar protesters caused their fallen comrades to "die for nothing"?

# Chapter 5

# American Youth and the Counterculture

**S**TUDENT ANTIWAR PROTESTS were part of a larger social movement called the counterculture. Many of the baby boomers who grew to young adulthood in the Vietnam era were questioning the values of the older generation. They believed that American society was too rigid and materialistic, focused on money and possessions instead of people. To these young people, the country's many problems—the Vietnam War, poverty, racism, the assassinations of John F. Kennedy, Robert Kennedy, and Dr. Martin Luther King, Jr.—were symptoms of a sick society in need of radical change.

The young showed their dissatisfaction by creating a new culture with values and customs that ran "counter" to those of traditional American society. Rebelling against the accepted rules of dress and behavior, counterculture youth grew their hair long and wore torn blue jeans, tie-dyed T-shirts, headbands and love beads, sandals or bare feet. "Hippies" turned their back on the "square," middle-class "Establishment" and experimented with different

American youth in the Vietnam era sought self-expression in many ways, including music, clothing, and jewelry and other ornaments.

lifestyles. Some moved to counterculture communities in large cities, especially Haight-Ashbury in San Francisco and Greenwich Village in New York; others joined farming communes where all shared equally in the labor and the possessions. Some experimented with "free love," meditation, Eastern religions, and vegetarian or natural-food diets. Many used mind-altering drugs, especially marijuana and the hallucinogenic drug LSD, to tune out society and "turn on" to an inner world.

Lifestyle and politics were intertwined in the counterculture movement. For countless young people who rebelled against contemporary society, opposing the war became a moral crusade. They marched in the front lines of antiwar protests. They also staged their own rallies promoting their ideals of peace and love. In January 1967, 20,000 "flower children" took part in the "World's First Human Be-In" at Haight-Ashbury, dancing, chanting, and ringing bells. During an October 1967 antiwar rally in Washington, some of the most far-out members of the counterculture stuck flowers in the rifles of soldiers guarding the Pentagon and tried to make the building rise into the air with mystical chants from an Eastern religion. But the height of the counterculture movement was the Woodstock festival. Gathering in a farm field in upstate New York in the summer of 1969, a half million young people celebrated what the *New York Times* called "a lifestyle that is its own declaration of independence."

Not all young people joined the counterculture movement, but all were touched by it in some way. A June 1969 poll showed that Americans under age thirty were more than four times as likely to have tried marijuana than older people. The poll also found that about three-quarters of the American public believed there was "a major generation gap" in the country. In a 1973 survey that looked at both college and noncollege youth, 90 percent of each group believed that "business is too concerned with profits," while 35 percent of each agreed with the statement "We are in a sick society."

## SDS Explains Why Youth Are Alienated

The basic philosophy of the counterculture movement was first spelled out by the Students for a Democratic Society (SDS). One of the most important student activist groups of the 1960s, SDS organized demonstrations on college campuses across the country. Its goals included reforming colleges and universities to make them more responsive to the needs of students, achieving equal rights for African Americans, ending the draft, and ending the Vietnam War. In 1962 SDS outlined its philosophy and guidelines for action in a document written by one of its leading figures, Tom Hayden, after a convention in Port Huron, Michigan. The "Port Huron Statement" maintained that the roots of young people's increasing sense of alienation could be found in the clash between the traditional American ideals of equality, freedom, and democracy and the realities of the country's racist, violent, and materialistic society. The statement proposed working through existing American institutions such as Congress and the political parties to create a just and open society "with the well-being and dignity of man as the essential measure of success." Seven years after the document was written, SDS lost much of its influence after the group split into several different factions, some favoring peaceful protests and others calling for more direct and, if necessary, violent action.

WE ARE PEOPLE OF THIS GENERATION, bred in at least modest comfort, housed now in universities, looking uncomfortably to the world
we inherit.

When we were kids the United States was the wealthiest and
strongest country in the world; the only one with the atom bomb, the
least scarred by modern war, an initiator of the United Nations that
we thought would distribute Western influence throughout the world.

Freedom and equality for each individual,
government of, by, and for the people—
these American values we found good,
principles by which we could live as men.
Many of us began maturing in complacency
[self-satisfaction].

*"The search for truly democratic alternatives . . . is a worthy and fulfilling human enterprise."*

As we grew, however, our comfort was
penetrated by events too troubling to dis-
miss. First, the permeating and victimizing
fact of human degradation, symbolized by the Southern struggle
against racial bigotry, compelled most of us from silence to activism.
Second, the enclosing fact of the Cold War, symbolized by the presence of the Bomb, brought awareness that we ourselves, and our
friends, and millions of abstract "others" we knew more directly
because of our common peril, might die at any time. . . .

While two-thirds of mankind suffers undernourishment, our own
upper classes revel amidst superfluous [excessive] abundance. . . .
Although mankind desperately needs revolutionary leadership, America
rests in national stalemate, its goals ambiguous [uncertain] and tradi-
tion-bound instead of informed and clear, its democratic system apa-
thetic and manipulated rather than "of, by, and for the people." . . .

Some would have us believe that Americans feel contentment amidst
prosperity—but might it not better be called a glaze above deeply felt
anxieties about their role in the new world? And if these anxieties pro-

Well-brought-up young ladies make their formal entry into society at a traditional debutante's ball in 1964—but in the words of a popular song of the day, "The times they are a-changin'."

duce a developed indifference to human affairs, do they not as well produce a yearning to believe there *is* an alternative to the present, that something *can* be done to change circumstances in the school, the workplaces, the bureaucracies, the government? It is to this latter yearning, at once the spark and engine of change, that we direct our present appeal. The search for truly democratic alternatives to the present, and a commitment to social experimentation with them, is a worthy and fulfilling human enterprise, one which moves us and, we hope, others today.

—From Tom Hayden, "Port Huron Statement," 1962.

## THINK ABOUT THIS

**1.** According to the document, what are the causes of young people's discontentment?

**2.** How might someone of the older generation answer the Port Huron Statement's criticisms?

**3.** In your opinion, does the document have relevance today? If so, how?

## College Graduates See a Future without Hope

College students led the way in the rebellion against the Establishment and experiments with alternative lifestyles. Having grown up in an era of prosperity, these young people took for granted what their parents and grandparents had strived for: a comfortable home, a good education, financial security. Freed from want, the young were able to look beyond material needs, to question the basic values of modern society, and to seek more from life. Concerns over social inequities and the Vietnam War led many to lose their respect for authority and their hope for the future. In this June 1968 graduation issue of the school newspaper of Brown University in Providence, Rhode Island, students explain why they are so dissatisfied with the world the older generation has left them.

COMMENCEMENT IS A TIME OF TRADITION. One of the most minor of these is the annual pilgrimage some *Herald* reporter makes to the deans' office so that the commencement issue can contain a rundown of the plans of graduating seniors.

This year, an interview with the deans would be ludicrous [ridiculous]. Only a few seniors can be sure of their own plans. However, every senior can be sure of [director of the draft] Lewis Hershey's plans. By the time school re-opens in the fall, more than half of this year's graduating seniors will be serving in the armed forces. By the next commencement, several of our number will be receiving their *Alumni Monthly* (it's like a class reunion twelve times a year) in Federal prison [for evading the draft]. Some will be dead.

It should come as no surprise to parents and alumni that the Class of '68 has lost hope in a power structure that sends so many of us so far to be killed for so little reason. Of course we are cynical. As peace candidates continue to do well in the primaries and opinion polls, both parties seem ready to nominate men pledged to continue our disastrous course in Asia. It was discouraging enough to work for [Eugene] McCarthy or [Robert] Kennedy when it seemed they had no chance of capturing popular support. But it is even more discouraging to see them capturing popular support while the Richard Nixons win the nominations. . . .

Of course we are bitter. All around us we see the cities burning while the nation's energies are expended for a cause we cannot believe in. . . .

We can't see why we should give the world the benefit of the doubt when that world seems so intent on destroying itself and us. We can't shrug things off because other generations had their problems, too; at least they could believe in the war they had to fight. We can't sit back and appreciate "how good we've got things" when by the most meaningful standards things aren't very good at all. We can't laugh it off when some of us are going to have to give our lives for reasons we cannot agree with.

The yellowed pages of this 1968 college newspaper still convey the anger and disillusionment of young Americans who saw the Vietnam War as a symptom of a sick society badly in need of change.

No doubt many parents and alumni, not to mention University officials, are unhappy with our attitude. They will be upset if our concerns spoil their graduation. Too bad; they are spoiling our world.

—*From the* Brown Daily Herald, *Providence, Rhode Island, June 2, 1968.*

## THINK ABOUT THIS

1. Who, besides Brown's students, is the intended audience for this article? What do you think the writers hoped to accomplish?
2. A common tactic in debating is to present the opponent's point of view and then try to prove it wrong. How do the writers use this tactic in the article? Do you think it makes their arguments more convincing?

# David Obst Remembers the "People's Park"

The gap between Establishment adults and counterculture youth led to a violent confrontation in Berkeley, California. The site of the main campus of the University of California, Berkeley was home to thousands of counterculture students, graduates, and dropouts. David Obst, who entered the university's graduate school in 1968, called Berkeley "the epicenter of the hippie world." Here Obst describes what happened in April 1969 when counterculture youth clashed with university officials over a three-acre "People's Park." The battle over the park lasted three days, with 9,000 people arrested, more than 150 injured, and one innocent bystander shot and killed.

PEOPLE'S PARK COULD BE VIEWED either as a spontaneous movement of the people of Berkeley to make a safe, green, improvement to their community, or the reckless takeover of private property by an anarchist band of street freaks. It kind of depended on how old you were.

Located just a tear gas canister shot away from the university, the park had been a three-acre muddy field the school had bought a couple of years before. In mid-April a number of street people decided the field would make a groovy park. They decided to reclaim the land from the university and give it back to the people. . . .

*"Wild in the streets again."*

For the next few weeks, hundreds of students and street people, folks who wouldn't work if their parents or employers begged or paid them, worked for free at the park. They transformed the mud-splattered field into a grass-covered park by bringing together a weird collection of sod, shrubs, and seedlings. A grove of apple trees was planted and a brick walkway was laid. Swings and a sandbox for kids were put up; there was even a fishpond, and my favorite feature, a "revolutionary cornfield," was planted. . . .

[*David goes on to recall the students' outrage when the university attempted to reclaim the park by surrounding it with a fence and posting No Trespassing signs. At a protest rally, speakers cried out against the "injustice of taking the park away from the people." Suddenly the crowd took to the streets on a mission to "liberate the park."*]

Thousands of us trotted toward the target. Crash! The front window of the Bank of America was broken. We were intoxicated by our own power. We ran headlong into a large group of police who guarded the park. A couple of kids turned on a fire hydrant and aimed the water at the cops. The crowd cheered. A few picked up rocks and tossed them at the police. The cops were not going to put up with that. Suddenly a massive barrage of tear gas was aimed at us. Wild in the streets again. . . .

The blue meanies lost it this time. They changed from firing tear gas to shooting shotguns loaded with no. 8 birdshot. They fired point-blank into the crowd. Kids went down. . . . My God, they were shooting at us. All we wanted was a place for kids to play—a park— and they were shooting at us. . . .

A couple thousand National Guardsmen arrived and a curfew was declared. The grown-ups had once again gone to war with their children.

—*From David Obst,* Too Good to Be Forgotten. *New York: John Wiley & Sons, 1998.*

## THINK ABOUT THIS

1. In your opinion, where do Obst's sympathies lie in this account—with the students or with the authorities?
2. Obst wrote this piece thirty years after the events he describes. How do you think the passage of time may have affected the way he tells his story?
3. Did the students and street people have a right to take over the park?

# A *Life* Poll Examines the Generation Gap

In May 1969 *Life,* one of the most popular and influential magazines of the Vietnam era, took an in-depth look at the generation gap. The magazine conducted a poll at one hundred high schools across the United States. Pollsters asked 2,500 students, parents, and teachers for their opinions on issues affecting their schools, such as whether students should have more say in the rules, discipline, and topics discussed in class. The results of the poll pointed out some of the areas of disagreement between the younger and older generations.

## STUDENT PARTICIPATION IN POLICY MAKING

|  | STUDENTS | PARENTS | TEACHERS |
| --- | --- | --- | --- |
| Want more | 58% | 20% | 35% |
| Want less | 2 | 11 | 4 |
| About same | 39 | 65 | 60 |
| Not sure | 1 | 4 | 1 |

## IMPORTANCE OF STUDENT PARTICIPATION IN POLICY MAKING

|  | STUDENTS | PARENTS | TEACHERS |
| --- | --- | --- | --- |
| Very important | 54% | 25% | 30% |
| Somewhat important | 34 | 38 | 39 |
| Not very important | 11 | 33 | 31 |
| Not sure | 1 | 4 | * |

*Less than 0.5%

In April 1968 students took over several buildings on the campus of Columbia University in New York City. Here protesters, making the peace sign, greet a professor—and the camera.

## SHOULD STUDENTS HAVE MORE SAY?

|  | STUDENTS | PARENTS | TEACHERS |
|---|---|---|---|
| In making rules . . . . . . . . . . . . . . . | 66% | 24% | 40% |
| In deciding curriculum . . . . . . . . . | 63 | 35 | 47 |
| In determining discipline of students. . | 48 | 28 | 37 |
| In deciding how to conduct classes . . . | 48 | 21 | 28 |
| In determination of grades . . . . . . . | 41 | 14 | 18 |

## SHOULD THESE TOPICS BE DISCUSSED IN CLASS?

|  | STUDENTS | PARENTS | TEACHERS |
|---|---|---|---|
| Folk rock music . . . . . . . . . . . . . . | 35% | 6% | 19% |
| Black students' rights . . . . . . . . . . | 52 | 27 | 36 |
| Underground paper and films . . . . . . | 40 | 17 | 36 |
| Sex hygiene. . . . . . . . . . . . . . . . . | 52 | 41 | 62 |
| Hair, dress, styles . . . . . . . . . . . . . | 37 | 30 | 28 |
| Use of drugs . . . . . . . . . . . . . . . . | 70 | 66 | 72 |

*—From "The Life Poll," Life magazine, May 16, 1969.*

## THINK ABOUT THIS

**1.** What is the greatest area of disagreement between students and both parents and teachers?

**2.** On which issues are students, parents, and teachers most in agreement?

# Country Joe McDonald Sings at Woodstock

Rock-and-roll was *the* music of the Vietnam generation. As a reporter for *Rolling Stone* magazine wrote, rock was viewed not just as entertainment but as "an essential component of a 'new culture,' along with drugs and radical politics." The ultimate joining of rock music and the counterculture was the Woodstock festival, held in New York's Catskill Mountain region in August 1969. Almost all of the top rock and pop music artists of the day performed at Woodstock, before a crowd made up of a half million young people high on music, drugs, peace, and love. A number of the songs performed, including Country Joe McDonald's "I-Feel-Like-I'm-Fixin'-to-Die-Rag," reflected the younger generation's frustration with the Vietnam War. McDonald's song became an anthem of the antiwar movement, sung by protesters at home as well as soldiers in Vietnam. The artist brought a special insight to this song. As a child he had watched his father, a member of the American Communist party, suffer emotional and financial hardships after being hounded by a government committee on un-American activities. At age seventeen McDonald enlisted in the U.S. Navy, where he served for three years, until 1962.

### I-FEEL-LIKE-I'M-FIXIN'-TO-DIE-RAG

> Yeah, come on all of you, big strong men.
> Uncle Sam needs your help again.
> He's got himself in a terrible jam.
> Way down yonder in Vietnam.
> So put down your books and pick up a gun.
> We're gonna have a whole lotta fun.
>
> *Refrain:*
> And it's one, two, three,
> What are we fightin' for?

Don't ask me, I don't give a damn.
Next stop is Vietnam;
And it's five, six, seven,
Open up the pearly gates,
Well, there ain't no time to wonder why,
Whoopee! we're all gonna die.

Huh! Well, come on, Wall Street and don't be slow.
Why man this is war a-go-go.
There's plenty good money to be made,
By supplying the army with the tools of the trade.
Just hope and pray if they drop the bomb,
They drop it on the Vietcong.

Concertgoers turn a stage scaffold into a jungle gym at Woodstock. The *New York Times* called the three-day rock festival a celebration of "a lifestyle that is its own declaration of independence."

*(Refrain)*

Well, come on Generals, let's move fast;
Your big chance has come at last.
Gotta go out and get those reds—
The only good commie is one who's dead.
And you know that peace can only be won,
When we've blown 'em all to kingdom come.

*(Refrain)*

Well, come on mothers throughout the land,
Pack your boys off to Vietnam.
Come on fathers, don't hesitate,
Send 'em off before it's too late.
Be the first one on your block
To have your boy come home in a box.

*(Refrain)*

—From "I-Feel-Like-I'm-Fixin'-to-Die-Rag," lyrics by Joe McDonald,
© 1965 renewed 1993 by Alkatraz Corner Music.

## THINK ABOUT THIS

1. How might McDonald's background have influenced him in writing this song?

2. Why do you think the song was popular with soldiers in Vietnam, who generally were angered by the antiwar movement?

This 1967 pamphlet cover illustrates a shift in the civil rights movement from nonviolent resistance to militant action. The pamphlet was distributed by the Student Non-Violent Coordinating Committee (SNCC), an organization originally founded to promote African-American voter registration in the South. The SNCC later reorganized as the radical Black Panther Party.

# Chapter 6

# The Battle for Civil Rights

**M**UCH OF THE INSPIRATION for nonviolent antiwar resistance came from the civil rights movement. African Americans had begun their struggle against segregation and injustice in the 1950s. At first, they concentrated on combating laws that permitted segregation in public schools. As the movement grew and organized, civil rights activists, including many young people both black and white, tried to force integration in other areas through peaceful demonstrations. They staged sit-ins and boycotts of libraries, theaters, lunch counters, and other public places in the American South that refused to serve blacks. They marched through southern cities and rallied in Washington, D.C. They organized "freedom rides" to protest segregated buses and bus terminals and ran voter registration drives for southern blacks. The leader in their campaign of nonviolent action was Dr. Martin Luther King, Jr., a young black minister who dreamed of a nation freed of prejudice, with equal rights and opportunities for all races.

By the mid-1960s, civil rights workers could point to some key victories. The most sweeping civil rights legislation in American history had been introduced by President Kennedy and signed into law by President Johnson in 1964. Meanwhile, Johnson's Great Society programs promised to wage "an unconditional war on poverty." But the pace of progress was slow. And as time passed, African Americans grew increasingly bitter as their peaceful protests were repeatedly answered with violence. Civil rights workers, including Dr. King, were harassed and jailed. Southern segregationists bombed and burned black people's homes, churches, and schools. Southern police used clubs, whips, cattle prods, and tear gas to break up civil rights demonstrations. Many young black activists began to question the movement's commitment to nonviolence. Trying to work peacefully within the white power structure had not brought justice, they argued. It was time to fight back with "black community power."

In August 1965 the cries of "Black Power" rang out in the Watts ghetto of Los Angeles, California. During the worst riot in American peacetime history, ten thousand black residents of Watts went on a six-day rampage of arson, looting, and violence. Over the next three summers, race riots raged in hundreds of other northern ghettos. The worst upheavals came in April 1968, after the assassination of Martin Luther King. In a sad and disturbing twist, the death of this great champion of nonviolence ignited riots in sixty-three cities, killing nearly fifty people, injuring thousands, and causing some sixty-seven million dollars in property damage.

By the time of his death, Dr. King had become an outspoken critic of the war in Vietnam. So had most other black leaders, both moderates and radicals. African Americans opposed the war because it drained money and attention from domestic programs to combat poverty. They also pointed to the fact that young black men were doing more than their fair share of the fighting and dying. To Black Power advocates, the Vietnam War looked like just another example of white America's racist policies. As militant civil rights leader Stokely Carmichael put it, U.S. involvement in Vietnam was a case of "white people sending black people to make war on yellow people in order to defend the land they stole from red people."

## Martin Luther King Opposes the Vietnam War

In the late 1950s Martin Luther King emerged as a leader of the civil rights movement. A southern Baptist minister with a moving, persuasive speaking style, King called for nonviolent action against racism and segregation. He organized peaceful marches, protests, and demonstrations for civil rights, including the March on Washington in August 1963. That landmark demonstration, the largest ever up to that time, brought a quarter of a million people of all races to the nation's capital to demand passage of a civil rights bill. An early supporter of U.S. policy in Vietnam, King gradually became convinced that America could not fight a war on two fronts: against communism abroad and poverty and racism at home. On April 4, 1967, in this sermon at New York City's Riverside Church, he added his voice to the antiwar movement. Exactly one year later, Martin Luther King was killed by an assassin's bullet in Memphis, Tennessee.

A TIME COMES WHEN silence is betrayal. That time has come for us in relation to Vietnam. . . .

A few years ago there was a shining moment [when] . . . it seemed as if there was a real promise of hope for the poor—both black and white—through the poverty program. There were experiments, hopes, new beginnings. Then came the buildup in Vietnam and I watched the program broken and eviscerated [gutted] as if it were some idle political plaything of a society gone mad on w . . . .

It became clear to me that the war was doing far more than devastating the hopes of the poor at home. It was sending their sons and their brothers and their husbands to fight and to die in extraordinarily high proportions relative to the rest of the population. We were taking the black young men who had been crippled by our society and sending them eight thousand miles away to guarantee liberties in Southeast Asia which they had not found in southwest Georgia and East Harlem. . . .

For the sake of those boys, for the sake of this government, for the sake of hundreds of thousands trembling under our violence, I cannot be silent.

*—From "Beyond Vietnam: A Time to Break Silence" by the Reverend Dr. Martin Luther King, Jr., April 4, 1967; reprinted in "Speeches of Dr. Martin Luther King, Jr.," National Park Service, U.S. Department of the Interior, at http://www.nps.gov/malu/documents/king_speeches.htm*

## THINK ABOUT THIS

1. What reasons does Dr. King give for changing his stand on the Vietnam War?
2. What do you think he means by the statement "silence is betrayal"?

## Malcolm X Speaks Out against Integration

As African Americans became increasingly impatient with the slow progress in their struggle for civil rights, some began to question the tactics and goals of moderate black leaders. One of the most powerful of the spokesmen for more radical action was Malcolm X. A minister in the Nation of Islam, or Black Muslim, religious movement, Malcolm X rejected the goal of integration. Instead, he called for the establishment of a separate black nation within the United States. In 1964 Malcolm X broke with the Black Muslims and formed his own more moderate organizations, committed to working within the political system to bring about social change. A year later he was assassinated, most likely by Black Muslim rivals. *The Autobiography of Malcolm X,* published soon after his death, included the following explanation of his opposition to integration.

NO *SANE* BLACK MAN REALLY WANTS INTEGRATION! No *sane* white man really wants integration! No sane black man really believes that the white man ever will give the black man anything more than token integration. . . .

As long as our people here in America are dependent upon the white man, we will always be begging him for jobs, food, clothing, and housing. And he will always control our lives, regulate our lives, and have the power to segregate us. . . .

The American black man should be focusing his every effort toward building his *own* businesses, and decent homes for himself. As other ethnic groups have done, let the black people, wherever possible, however possible, patronize their own kind, hire their own kind, and start in those ways to build up the black race's ability to do for itself. That's the only way the American black man is ever going to get respect. One thing the white man never can give the black man is self-respect! The black man never can become independent and recognized as a human being who is truly equal with other human beings until he has what they have, and until he is doing for himself what others are doing for themselves. . . .

I'm right *with* the Southern white man who believes that you can't have so-called "integration," at least not for long, without intermarriage increasing. And what good is this for anyone? Let's again face reality. In a world as color-hostile as this, man or woman, black or white, what do they want with a mate of the other race?

*"One thing the white man never can give the black man is self-respect!"*

Certainly white people have served enough notice of their hostility to any blacks in their families and neighborhoods. And the way most Negroes feel today, a mixed couple probably finds that black families, black communities are even more hostile than the white ones. So what's bound to face "integrated" marriages, except being unwelcomed, unwanted "misfits" in whichever world they try to live in? What we arrive at is that "integration," socially, is no good for either side. "Integration," ultimately, would destroy the white race . . . and destroy the black race.

Malcolm X at a Black Muslim rally in New York City, August 1963

—*From Malcolm X and Alex Haley,* The Autobiography of Malcolm X. *New York: Random House, 1965.*

## THINK ABOUT THIS

1. What reasons does Malcolm X give for rejecting the goal of integration?
2. What does he urge black people to do to improve their lives?
3. Do you agree or disagree with his statements?

## The Black Panthers Give a Lesson in Politics

In the summer of 1965, a civil rights organization called the Student Non-Violent Coordinating Committee (SNCC) began a drive to register black voters in Lowndes County, Alabama. Lowndes County was typical of many communities in the Deep South—although blacks greatly outnumbered whites, the county's white residents had long used tactics such as literacy tests to prevent black residents (many of whom were uneducated) from registering to vote. SNCC workers planned to register enough black voters to establish a new political party, which could then put up its own candidates for county offices, allowing blacks to gain control of their local government. In 1966 the new party, named the Lowndes County Freedom Organization, distributed a pamphlet that urged blacks to exercise their right to vote, even in the face of violence and harassment. One part of the pamphlet, reproduced below, detailed the tactics that had been used to keep blacks from voting. The organization that worked so hard for voting rights would soon become better known as the Black Panther Party, named for the fierce black cat pictured on its pamphlets and posters. The Black Panthers developed into one of the most influential African American organizations calling for Black Power and armed resistance to white oppression.

## WHAT IS POLITICS?

Politics is the coming together of people to make decisions about their lives. For example, who is going to be sheriff, who will be elected to the school board, who will be the mayor of your city. However, in the past, Negroes have not been permitted to practice politics. A few people, most of them white, have worked in politics to benefit themselves.

## HOW HAVE WE BEEN KEPT OUT OF POLITICS?

1. Certain laws and practices have kept Negroes from voting.
2. Negroes have been kept out of political parties.
3. Negroes have been beaten when they tried to register to vote, and told time and time again that politics and voting were "white folks' business."
4. They have told us that we are not "qualified" to practice politics, that we are not "qualified" to run our own lives! Everyone knows if he will think about it that each and every grown man and woman is just as "qualified" as anyone else to decide what he wants his life to be like. There may be some information that some of us need in order to decide how to go about making our lives what we want them to be, but we can get that information and we can learn it just as well as anyone else can.
5. They have told us that Negroes "just can't stick together."

## WHY COME TOGETHER?

When you come together you can determine who from your own community can do the thing you want done. If you don't come together, the people who have been running the show will put their own candidates up and vote for programs that will benefit them only and you will have no say at all. . . .

## NOW IS THE TIME!

If ever there was a time for Negroes to leave the white supremacy Democratic Party of Alabama alone—now is the time!
If ever we had a chance to do something about the years of low pay, beatings, burnings of homes, denial of the right to vote, bad education and washed-out roads—now is the time!

—From the Lowndes County Freedom Organization voting pamphlet, 1966.

1. What are the short-term (immediate) and long-term goals of the pamphlet writers?
2. Why do you think it was important for the organization to use an easy-to-recognize symbol on printed materials for the county's black residents? Why do you think the symbol of a black panther was chosen?

## Mississippi Activists Say Blacks Should Refuse to Serve in Vietnam

In May 1965 public opinion polls showed that black Americans were 50 percent more likely than whites to oppose the Vietnam War. African Americans were concerned that the war was taking away funds from antipoverty programs. They also knew that black soldiers were far more likely than whites to be sent on dangerous combat assignments in Vietnam. In fact, while African Americans made up about 10 percent of U.S. troops in Vietnam in 1965, they accounted for more than 20 percent of combat deaths. Some black leaders urged young African American men to refuse to serve in what they considered a white racist war. The McComb, Mississippi, branch of the Freedom Democratic Party, a political organization established by the SNCC, circulated an antiwar petition that included this explanation of its stand against service in Vietnam.

Here are five reasons why Negroes should not be in any war fighting for America:

1. No Mississippi Negroes should be fighting in Vietnam for the White Man's freedom, until all the Negro People are free in Mississippi.

2. Negro boys should not honor the draft here in Mississippi. Mothers should encourage their sons not to go.

3. We will gain respect and dignity as a race only by forcing the United States Government and the Mississippi Government to come with guns, dogs, and trucks to take our sons away to fight and be killed protecting Mississippi, Alabama, Georgia, and Louisiana.

4. No one has a right to ask us to risk our lives and kill other Colored People in . . . Vietnam, so that the White American can get richer. We will be looked upon as traitors by all the Colored People of the world if the Negro people continue to fight and die without a cause.

*" . . . Negro people continue to fight and die without a cause."*

5. Last week a White soldier from New Jersey was discharged from the Army because he refused to fight in Vietnam and went on a hunger strike. Negro boys can do the same thing. We can write and ask our sons if they know what they are fighting for. If he answers Freedom, tell him that's what we are fighting for here in Mississippi. And if he says Democracy tell him the truth—we don't know anything about Communism, socialism, and all that, but we do know that Negroes have caught hell here under this *American Democracy.*

*—From the McComb, Mississippi, Freedom Democratic Party antiwar petition, July 1965.*

## THINK ABOUT THIS

1. Compare this document with the antiwar petition on page 30. How are the two documents similar? How are they different?

2. What two groups are the main audience for this petition? What do the petition writers want each group to do?

## A Black Veteran Recalls Racial Tensions in the Infantry

Racial tensions on the American home front also affected servicemen and women in Vietnam. Black and white GIs served in integrated units. When they were out in the field, where they depended on one another for survival, racial conflicts were few. But when the men returned to their base camps to rest up between missions, blacks and whites often separated into hostile factions. Radical black soldiers adopted the look and manners of the Black Power movement, growing Afro hairstyles, wearing medallions and clothes with militant symbols and slogans, and developing their own complex hand signals and slang. Some whites flew Confederate flags and hurled racial insults; a few put on Ku Klux Klan

African-American GIs in Vietnam greet one another with clenched fists, symbolizing black power.

outfits after the assassination of Martin Luther King. Fights often broke out between blacks and whites, sometimes with fists, sometimes with knives or guns. Richard Ford, who served with the 25th Infantry Division from 1967 to 1968, describes what happened on one occasion when his unit returned from a search-and-destroy mission to its base camp at Nha Trang, on the South China Sea.

THE RACIAL INCIDENTS didn't happen in the field. Just when we went to the back. It wasn't so much that they were against us. It was just that we felt that we were being taken advantage of, 'cause it seemed like more blacks in the field than in the rear.

In the rear we saw a bunch of rebel flags. They didn't mean nothing by the rebel flag. It was just saying we for the South. It didn't mean that they hated blacks. But after you in the field, you took the flags very personally.

One time we saw these flags in Nha Trang on the MP barracks. They was playing hillbilly music. Had their shoes off dancing. Had nice, pretty bunks. Mosquito nets over top the bunks. . . . Air conditioning. Cement floors. We just came out the jungles. We dirty, we smelly, hadn't shaved. We just went off. Said, "Y'all the real enemy. We stayin' here." We turned the bunks over, started tearing up the stereo. They just ran out. Next morning, they shipped us back up.

**MP**
*military police*

In the field, we had the utmost respect for each other, because when a fire fight is going on and everybody is facing north, you don't want to see nobody looking around south. If you was a member of the Ku Klux Klan, you didn't tell nobody.

—*From Wallace Terry,* Bloods: An Oral History of the Vietnam War by Black Veterans. *New York: Random House, 1984.*

## THINK ABOUT THIS

1. Why do you think the black soldiers reacted as they did to the rebel flags?

2. Richard Ford's narrative comes from a collection of oral histories by black veterans. What qualities do oral histories have that make them different from written histories? Do you think one of these forms of history is more accurate or more enjoyable to read than the other?

During the turbulent Vietnam years, women staged marches, sit-ins, and
strikes to demand equality in work, education, and the law.

# Chapter 7

# The Women's Liberation Movement

**M**ILLIONS OF AMERICAN WOMEN took part in the civil rights movement and spoke out on one side or the other of the conflict over the Vietnam War. At the same time, women were fighting a battle all their own, for legal and social equality in a "man's world."

Ever since the country's founding, there have been feminists who campaigned for women's rights—for fair employment and property laws, for equal access to education, for the right to vote. Through the years these women made great strides. But by the 1960s, American women were still being treated like second-class citizens in many ways. Most women who worked outside the home had low-paying jobs as waitresses, maids, sales clerks, or secretaries. So-called protective labor laws barred them from higher-paying occupations considered physically or morally hazardous, such as truck driving or bartending. Even women who managed to climb the career ladder—lawyers, scientists, college professors—were paid less than men doing the same work. Also, in many states, various regulations prohibited women from renting a hotel room or an apartment on their own, from entering a bar or restaurant without a male escort, from starting a business or opening a credit account without their husband's consent. According to the image presented by popular magazines, movies, and TV, women were the "weaker" sex, meant to find their true fulfillment in the home, as perfect—and perfectly content—wives and mothers.

Resentful and unhappy with all these restrictions, women were ripe for a revolution. The spark that set them off was the 1964 best-seller *The Feminine Mystique* by journalist Betty Friedan. The book exploded the myth of the "happy homemaker," reporting that vast numbers of women were deeply dissatisfied with their limited roles and choices in life. Thousands of women wrote to thank Friedan for putting into words feelings they had been unable or afraid to express. They began talking to one another and speaking out for change. And in the climate of protest and social activism that characterized the Vietnam era, a new women's rights movement was born.

In 1966 Betty Friedan and other feminist leaders founded the National Organization for Women (NOW) to lead the fight for women's rights. NOW battled sex discrimination in the workplace, forcing employers to open male-only jobs to women. It campaigned for equal pay for men and women doing the same work. The organization also persuaded Congress to pass the Equal Rights Amendment, a proposed amendment to the Constitution outlawing discrimination on account of sex.

By the early 1970s, millions of women belonged to NOW or to one of the many smaller women's liberation groups founded in communities all over the country. These new feminists tackled sex discrimination in local schools, businesses, and government. They started women's health clinics and self-defense classes, shelters for battered wives, and day-care centers for the children of working mothers. Sometimes they joined forces in rallies for equality. The largest of these took place on August 26, 1970, the fiftieth anniversary of the passage of the Nineteenth Amendment, which gave women the vote. Hundreds of thousands of women in nearly every major city took to the streets in the Women's Strike for Equality Day demonstrations. When New York City officials refused to close off Fifth Avenue for the feminist demonstrators, 50,000 women linked hands or arms and marched anyway. "We marched, in great swinging long lines, from sidewalk to sidewalk," recalled Betty Friedan, "and the police on their horses got out of our way."

## Florynce Kennedy Talks to *Life* about the Women's Movement

In September 1970, following the Women's Strike for Equality Day demonstrations, *Life* magazine looked at the women's liberation movement. *Life's* editors reported on the "long and painful record of little progress in a man's world" and interviewed "eight women who succeeded in it." One of these women was Florynce Kennedy, a prominent African-American lawyer who was a long-time supporter of women's liberation and the civil rights movement.

WOMEN HAVE BEEN IN A LOT of the recent movements and have begun to see the way men treat them. They've started saying, "Look at this.

Men make all the decisions and we have to be second-class." I feel that women have to be against men for the same reason that black people have to be against white people. Men are agents for the system. The average person who is oppressed feels that he or she is the reason for their own oppression. So if they're black they think, well, you know, being black is really kind of a terrible thing. I think that women have felt they were to blame for whatever their circumstances were. To whatever extent they were damaged, they felt it was a personal thing—that their husband was the problem, rather than the institution of marriage.

*"... women have to let this system know they don't like it!"*

Whatever your reason, accepting your status is the reason society can continue. The society can be stopped cold dead if everybody resists oppression. That's why strikes are good. They are symbolic.

I urge that when women strike we don't make deposits at the bank. I urge that we don't buy anything. I urge that we don't have just one women's strike but that women select one day a month, or a week, to assert their position. Women have accepted oppression for so long that it's extremely important to make it clear they are not going to accept it any longer. When you spit on a person, you're not trying to drown him; you're just trying to let him know that you don't like him. And women have to let this system know they don't like it!

—From "Women Arise: The Revolution That Will Affect
Everybody," *Life*, September 4, 1970

## THINK ABOUT THIS

1. What comparisons does Kennedy make between the women's liberation and civil rights movements?

2. What does she recommend women do to combat sex discrimination?

# Congress Passes the Equal Rights Amendment

A Constitutional amendment guaranteeing women equal rights under the law was introduced in every session of Congress from 1923 to 1972. Finally, the U.S. House of Representatives and the Senate passed the Equal Rights Amendment (ERA). On March 22, 1972, Congress sent the proposed Twenty-Seventh Amendment to the state legislatures, with a seven-year deadline for ratification by three-quarters (thirty-eight) of the states. Within two years thirty states had voted their approval. But in the mid-1970s a strong opposition movement organized to defeat the amendment. ERA supporters persuaded Congress to extend the ratification deadline to 1982. Nevertheless, when the final deadline was reached, the ERA "died," still three states short of being ratified and enacted into law.

*Resolved by the Senate and House of Representatives of the United States of America in Congress assembled (two-thirds of each House concurring therein),* that the following article is proposed as an amendment to the Constitution of the United States, which shall be valid to all intents and purposes as part of the Constitution when ratified by the legislatures of three-fourths of the several States within seven years from the date of its submission by the Congress:

*"Equality of rights under the law shall not be denied . . . on account of sex."*

SECTION 1. Equality of rights under the law shall not be denied or abridged by the United States or by any State on account of sex.

SECTION 2. The Congress shall have the power to enforce,
by appropriate legislation, the provisions of this
article.

SECTION 3. This amendment shall take effect two years
after the date of ratification.

*—From the "Equal Rights" Amendment as introduced to Congress*
*in 1971,* Proposed Amendments to the Constitution of the United States,
Congressional Research Service Report 85-36, Washington, 1985.

## THINK ABOUT THIS

**1.** Why do you think the ERA passed Congress in 1972 after failing to
pass for forty-eight years?

**2.** Why do you think Congress attaches deadlines for ratification of most
Constitutional amendments? Do you think this is a fair and reasonable
practice?

## Gloria Steinem Defends the ERA

Gloria Steinem was one of the "founding mothers" of the feminist
movement. As a young journalist in the 1960s, Steinem investigated
cases of sex discrimination and wrote articles in support of
women's rights, the rights of migrant farm workers, and the antiwar
movement. In 1971 Steinem joined with Betty Friedan and other
feminist leaders to organize the National Women's Political Caucus,
an organization supporting political candidates who fought for
women's interests. That same year she founded *Ms.*, a popular magazine that soon became the "bible of the feminist movement." Following is an excerpt from Steinem's testimony at Senate committee
hearings during the debate over the Equal Rights Amendment.

I AM HERE IN SUPPORT of the equal rights amendment. . . .

During 12 years of working for a living, I have experienced much of the legal and social discrimination reserved for women in this country. I have been refused service in public restaurants, ordered out of public gathering places, and turned away from apartment rentals; all for the clearly-stated, sole reason that I am a woman. And all without the legal remedies available to blacks and other minorities. I have been excluded from professional groups, writing assignments on so-called "unfeminine" subjects such as politics, full participation in the Democratic Party, jury duty, and even from such small male privileges as discounts on airline fares. Most important to me, I have been denied a society in which women are encouraged, or even allowed to think of themselves as first-class citizens and responsible human beings.

*"We have all been silent for too long."*

However, after 2 years of researching the status of American women, I have discovered that in reality, I am very, very lucky. Most women, both wage-earners and housewives, routinely suffer more humiliation and injustice than I do.

As a freelance writer, I don't work in the male-dominated hierarchy of an office. . . . I am not one of the millions of women who must support a family. Therefore, I haven't had to go on welfare because there are no day-care centers for my children while I work, and I haven't had to submit to the humiliating welfare inquiries about my private and sexual life, inquiries from which men are exempt. I haven't had to brave the sex bias of labor unions and employers, only to see my family subsist on a median [average] salary 40 percent less than the male median salary.

I hope this committee will hear the personal, daily injustices suffered by many women—professionals and day laborers, women housebound by welfare as well as by suburbia. We have all been silent for too long. But we won't be silent anymore.

*—From Dr. Catharine Stimpson and the Congressional Information Service,* Women and the "Equal Rights" Amendment: Senate Subcommittee Hearings on the Constitutional Amendment, 91st Congress. *New York: R. R. Bowker, 1972.*

## THINK ABOUT THIS

1. What examples does Steinem give of sex discrimination that she has personally experienced? That other women have experienced?
2. How might a Constitutional amendment guaranteeing "equality of rights under the law" affect those types of discrimination? Could it guarantee that such discrimination would never occur again?

# Phyllis Schlafly Defines a Successful Marriage

Opponents of the feminist movement accused the "women's libbers" of being loud, pushy, and "unladylike" and urged women to return to their traditional roles. According to "antifeminist" leader Phyllis Schlafly, the Equal Rights Amendment was an "assault on the role of the American woman as wife and mother, and on the family as the basic unit of society." Schlafly and her supporters argued that if the ERA became law, a variety of disasters would follow: men would no longer support their families, pregnant women would be drafted and sent into combat, men and women would be forced to share public toilets. In 1973 Schlafly founded STOP ERA, a group that coordinated efforts by conservative women across the country to prevent ratification by their state legislatures. While the anti-ERA groups were strong and united, the pro-ERA forces were made up of feminists from many different women's organizations, often with different beliefs and goals. In the end the antifeminists were victorious, and the ERA was defeated. Schlafly went on to write several books, including *The Power of the Positive Woman,* which included this explanation of her views on the proper roles of husbands and wives in marriage.

Phyllis Schlafly led conservative Americans in a successful drive to stop ratification of the Equal Rights Amendment.

ANY SUCCESSFUL VEHICLE must have one person at the wheel with ultimate responsibility. When I fly on a plane or sail on a ship, I'm glad there is one captain who has the final responsibility and can act decisively in a crisis situation. A family cannot be run by committee. . . .

Every successful country and company has one "chief executive officer." None successfully functions with responsibility equally divided between cochairmen or copresidents. The United States has a president and a vice president. They are not equal. The vice president supports and carries out the policies enunciated [spelled out] by the president. Likewise with the presidents and vice-presidents of all business concerns. Vice-presidents can and do have areas of jurisdiction delegated to them, but there is always one final decision maker. The experience of the ages has taught us that this system is sound, practical, and essential for success. The republic of ancient Rome tried a system of two consuls of equal authority, and it failed.

*"A family cannot be run by committee."*

If marriage is to be a successful institution, it must likewise have an ultimate decision maker, and that is the husband. Seen in this light, the laws that give the husband the right to establish the domicile [dwelling place] of the marriage and to give his surname to his children are good laws designed to keep the family together. They are not anachronisms from a bygone era from which wives should be liberated in the name of equality. . . . That "equal right" is simply incompatible with a happy lifetime marriage.

*—From Phyllis Schlafly,* The Power of the Positive Woman.
*New York: Random House, 1977.*

## THINK ABOUT THIS

**1.** To what three things does Schlafly compare marriage? Do you find her comparisons and the conclusions she draws from them convincing?

**2.** Like Schlafly, many of the most outspoken antifeminists were women. Why do you think this was the case?

## Rose Sandecki Serves in Vietnam

More than 7,500 American women served with the U.S. military in Vietnam, and thousands more worked with the Red Cross and other volunteer organizations supporting the servicemen. While their sisters fought for women's rights and other causes on the home front, these women faced danger every day in a deadly conflict thousands of miles from home. The vast majority of military women in Vietnam were nurses. Few were prepared for the war's endless horror show of massive wounds, infections, pain, and death. Rose Sandecki, an army nurse and captain who served in Vietnam from 1968 to 1969, describes the emotional wall most women built up to deal with the constant stress and danger.

WHEN I LOOK BACK ON IT, I was naive when I walked through those doors. I learned a lot very quickly, seeing the types of casualties and the numbers of them. They were all so young. Seeing this on a daily basis twelve to fourteen hours a day, six or seven days a week, I think that I became somewhat callous and bitter. . . .

*" . . . it was sort of a skin protecting me from what was going on."*

The way of dealing with the sheer amount of patients, the long hours in the hospital, was by putting up a wall, the emotional numbing that we talk about. I think it built up over a period of time. Each day I went in and the more I saw, the thicker this wall became; it was sort of a skin protecting me from what was going on. . . .

I got a phone call on the ward from the chief nurse, saying, "You've got a patient there that is going to get an award. Make sure that the bed has clean sheets, the area is straightened up, and the ward looks good." Which really turned me off to begin with: Let's clean up the ward because we've got VIPs coming in. Well, the VIP happened to be the general of the 25th Infantry Division along with his aide and an entourage of about twelve people. And this patient, when he came through the recovery room the day before, had remembered

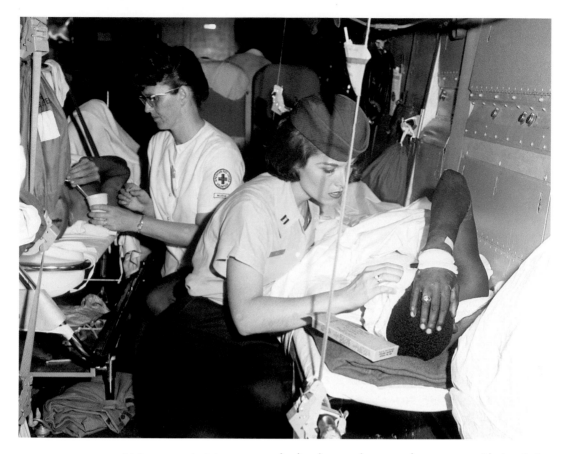

U.S. nurses in Vietnam worked at hospitals in combat areas and behind the lines. Eight nurses died in the line of duty.

**frag wounds**
*injuries caused by "fragments" of a bomb or grenade*

me. This was his second visit to us. He had been there three months before with frag wounds, had been sent back to the jungle, and came back this time with both of his legs blown off—he was all of about twenty years old. . . . The entourage was coming to give him an award because he happened to be number twenty thousand to come through the 12th Evac [Evacuation] Hospital. In 1968 there were twenty-four Army evac hospitals in Vietnam, and he was number *twenty thousand* through *one* of twenty-four Army hospitals. . . . So, for this distinction, the general comes in and gives him a watch. They have this little ceremony, give him a Purple Heart and the watch. I'm standing off in the corner watching all this, and as the general handed him the watch—"From the 25th Infantry Division as a token of our appreciation"—the kid more or less flings the watch back at him and says something like, "I can't accept this, sir; it's not going to help me walk." I couldn't really see the expression on the general's face, but they all left after this little incident. I went over and just put my arms around him and hugged him. . . . I started crying . . . and I think he was crying. I really admired him for that. That was one time that I let the feelings down and let somebody see what I felt. It took a lot for him to do that, and it sort of said what this war was all about to me.

—*From Keith Walker,* A Piece of My Heart: The Stories of Twenty-Six American Women Who Served in Vietnam. *Novato, CA: Presidio Press, 1985.*

## THINK ABOUT THIS

**1.** Why do you think this patient's actions broke through Sandecki's emotional wall?

**2.** What do you think the war "was all about" to Sandecki?

# Chapter 8

# The Credibility Gap

**D**URING THE VIETNAM ERA, many Americans lost faith and confidence in their government and its leaders. Military and government officials repeatedly misled the public, concealing or distorting the truth about U.S. operations in Vietnam. The difference between what these officials said and what was actually true—and the loss of trust caused by that difference—became known as the credibility gap.

The credibility gap first emerged among American journalists in Vietnam. In the early years of the war, journalists were told that U.S. forces were only advising the South Vietnamese, but they could see that Americans were fighting and dying. While U.S. officials praised South Vietnamese President Ngo Dinh Diem as a democratic and popular leader, the reporters found him corrupt, repressive, and out of touch with his people. Battles lost by South Vietnamese forces were called victories. Enemy body counts were grossly inflated. All the contradictions between what journalists saw in Vietnam and what they were told were so glaring that the reporters gave the daily news conferences held by U.S. military

President Richard Nixon waves good-bye from the steps of Marine One after leaving the White House for the final time, August 9, 1974. Nixon's role in the Watergate scandal had forced him to resign rather than face impeachment.

spokespersons in Saigon a grimly humorous name: the "Five O'Clock Follies."

Americans on the home front were troubled, too. Official government reports on the war didn't seem to match what they read in their newspapers and saw on TV. Month after month U.S. leaders issued optimistic reports of "steady progress" in Vietnam. Meanwhile, the war dragged on and American casualties continued to rise. In late 1967 the Johnson administration launched a massive public relations campaign, producing charts, graphs, and documents to prove that the enemy was "certainly losing" and the end of the war had "come into view." A few months later, the Tet Offensive made those claims look like lies, further shattering public confidence.

In 1969 Americans learned that the Nixon administration had ordered secret, possibly illegal bombing attacks on Communist positions in neutral Cambodia. Two years later, the *New York Times* published the Pentagon Papers, a series of top-secret documents revealing government deceptions about U.S. policy in Southeast Asia dating all the way back to the 1940s. But the most devastating revelations came in 1973. That year the Watergate scandal disclosed a tangled trail of government crimes and cover-ups, with President Nixon himself at the heart of the conspiracy. Watergate stunned the nation, toppled the president, and dealt yet another blow to Americans' faith in the truthfulness of their leaders. The scandal also had an effect on Vietnam and future wars. During the Watergate investigations, Nixon's political power fell to an all-time low. Congress took advantage of that situation to pass a bill that limited a president's authority to commit troops to foreign conflicts.

# President Johnson Sees No "Way of Winning" in Vietnam

President Lyndon Johnson was determined not to let the Communists take over South Vietnam. At the same time, he was afraid that dramatically increasing the war effort—using massive military force to defeat North Vietnam—would turn the American people and Congress against him, eroding support for his Great Society programs. So the president chose a middle course: he escalated the war gradually, using American military might to keep hammering the Communists in the hope that they would abandon their aggression in South Vietnam. As Johnson turned up the pressure, he also tried to manage public opinion. But his efforts backfired. By telling the American people as little as possible about the U.S. buildup and painting an overly optimistic picture of the prospects for victory, he contributed to an ever-widening credibility gap. The following excerpts come from tape recordings of phone conversations between the president and his advisers about the start of the Rolling Thunder bombing campaign in early 1965. In these conversations Johnson rehearses the arguments his administration will use to maintain that the bombings are not an escalation of the war.

*THURSDAY, FEBRUARY 25, 1965, 10:30 A.M.*

> JOHNSON: I want to be very careful that we don't show that we are desperate and dramatic and we are changing our policy.
> SECRETARY OF STATE DEAN RUSK: Right.

**B-57s**
*bomber airplanes*

**Pathfinders**
*infantrymen who locate landing sites for U.S. aircraft in enemy territory*

JOHNSON: All of TV now is trying to say that this a big escalation, and that the B-57s yesterday are an entirely new policy. I've made clear to the people I've talked to . . . that the congressional resolution [the Gulf of Tonkin Resolution] . . . says that we will reply to any attacks and we will deter any aggression. . . . Now, when we could deter it with helicopters, we did. When we could deter it with shots from the Vietnamese troops, we did. When we could prevent aggression with Pathfinders and sending one of our planes in to lead their planes with their Air Force, we did. . . . As [the Vietcong] stepped up and . . . tied down our Ranger companies, we did not change our policy, we changed our equipment.

RUSK: That's right.

JOHNSON: Because they escalated. They brought in the ships with all the guns, and they brought in a lot more people. The infiltration increased, and they had their staging areas, and we had Ranger companies tied down there, and it was going to cost hundreds of thousands of Vietnamese lives.

RUSK: Right.

JOHNSON: So, at the request of the South Vietnamese government, we busted 'em up and released those people and saved their lives with the B-57s. Now, it is true that this is probably the first time that the B-57's been used in South Vietnam. But the Congress authorized us and directed us to prevent aggression, and we have not changed our policy. That is our policy. That *resolution* is our policy. That *is* our authority. . . .

RUSK: Right.

JOHNSON: . . . I think that what they're going to try to put in our lap is that we're the warmongers, and we're changing our policy, that we've got a brand-new policy from day to day, we've really got no policy at all. . . . That's the commentators' line. I think this is the answer to it.

*"I want to be very careful that we don't show that we are desperate."*

*FRIDAY, FEBRUARY 26, 1965, 9:00 A.M.*

SECRETARY OF DEFENSE ROBERT MCNAMARA: We have rescheduled the strike for tonight. The weather outlook is still bad. Whether it will come off or not, we don't know. The commanders from the field are in with unanimous recommendations that we move a portion of a Marine Expeditionary Brigade into Da Nang to provide protection there. The build-up of Vietcong forces in the surrounding area is fairly substantial, and they're fearful that the huge number of aircraft we have in Da Nang and the personnel are subject to attack. This is a recommendation I would be very reluctant to accept, but frankly I doubt we have any alternative. . . .

JOHNSON: . . . I think that we ought to try to figure out what we can do. Now, we're off to bombing these people. We're over that hurdle, and I don't think anything is going to be as bad as

losing, and I don't see any way of winning. . . . I do think that this bombing in South Vietnam has added something. . . . I'm scared to death of putting ground forces in, but I'm *more* frightened about losing a bunch of planes from lack of security.

—From Conversations 6885 and 6887,
"LBJ White House Tapes,"
at http://www.c-span.org/lbj

Recently released tape recordings of President Lyndon Johnson's White House phone conversations are a valuable primary source for students of American history. The tapes reveal the inner workings of the Johnson presidency, including his private doubts about the chances of victory in Vietnam.

1. According to President Johnson, what arguments should the administration use to answer charges that the bombing campaign escalated the war? Where does he indicate that he might privately believe it *is* an escalation?

2. If you have access to the Internet, you can listen to these conversations (http://www.c-span.org/lbj ). Tapes are also available through the LBJ Library and Museum, 2313 Red River Street, Austin, TX 78705 (512-916-5137). Does hearing the actual conversations change your impressions about what the president and his aides are saying?

## A GI Sets the Scene for the My Lai Massacre

In November 1969 investigative reporter Seymour Hersh broke the story of a brutal massacre of South Vietnamese civilians by American troops in the village of My Lai (pronounced "me lie"). More than a year earlier, on March 16, 1968, an infantry platoon searching for Vietcong guerrillas in the village had run wild, rounding up and slaughtering an estimated five hundred old men, women, and children. A number of higher officers who knew about the atrocities kept silent. After a serviceman who had heard about My Lai wrote to his congressman, however, the army began a secret investigation of the incident. Eventually thirteen officers and enlisted men were charged with war crimes. The platoon's leader, Lieutenant William Calley, was convicted and sentenced to life imprisonment but released after three years. The My Lai atrocities added to the growing opposition to the war and to the suspicion that a wide gap existed between government reports and what was really going on in Vietnam. In this letter Gregory Olsen, one of the soldiers in Calley's platoon who refused to participate in the My Lai killings, describes incidents that took place two days earlier.

*[MARCH 14, 1968]*

Dear Dad:

How's everything with you?

I'm still on the bridge, we leave here Saturday.

One of our platoons went out on a routine patrol today and came across a 155-mm artillery round that was booby trapped. It killed one man, blew the legs off two others, and injured two more.

And it all turned out a bad day made even worse. On their way back to [camp] they saw a woman working in the fields. They shot and wounded her. Then they kicked her to death and emptied their magazines in her head. They slugged every little kid they came across.

*magazines* ammunition chambers

Why in God's name does this have to happen? These are all seemingly normal guys; some were friends of mine. For a while they were like wild animals.

It was murder, and I'm ashamed of myself for not trying to do anything about it.

This isn't the first time, Dad. I've seen it many times before. I don't know why I'm telling you all this; I guess I just want to get it off my chest.

My faith in my fellow men is shot all to hell. I just want the time to pass and I just want to come home. . . .

*N.V.A.* North Vietnamese Army

Saturday we're going to be dropped by air in an N.V.A. stronghold [My Lai]. . . .

I love and miss you and Mom so much—
Your son,
*Greg*

—From Seymour M. Hersh, My Lai 4: A Report on the Massacre and Its Aftermath. *New York: Random House, 1970.*

1. Compare this letter with the one by George Olsen (no relation) on page 15. How are the experiences described by the two men similar and how are they different? What might explain the difference in the way the men in the two platoons treated civilians?

2. Does the fact that the Americans were fighting a guerrilla war in any way explain or excuse their actions at My Lai? In the view of the military court, how responsible were the soldiers?

## The *New York Times* Defends Publication of the Pentagon Papers

In June 1971 the *New York Times* began publishing excerpts from the secret government study known as the Pentagon Papers. The forty-seven-volume study had been stolen and leaked to the press by a former Defense Department employee, Daniel Ellsberg. It included government documents tracing the history of American involvement in Vietnam from 1945 to 1968. These reports showed that for decades U.S. leaders had deliberately misled the American public, covering up questionable or illegal actions in Vietnam and promising early success while planning for a long, costly fight. After the Nixon administration won a court order temporarily halting publication of the Pentagon Papers, the *Times* responded with the following editorial. Two weeks later, the Supreme Court ruled that the Constitution's guarantee of freedom of the press gave the paper the right to publish the documents. Nixon's attempts to suppress the Pentagon Papers only added to the public's suspicion that the government was still lying about Vietnam.

*"... it is in the interest of the people of this country to be informed."*

*JUNE 16, 1971*

In an unprecedented example of censorship, the Attorney General of the United States has temporarily succeeded in preventing The New York Times from continuing to publish documentary and other material taken from a secret Pentagon study of the decisions affecting American participation in the Vietnam War. . . .

What was the reason that impelled The Times to publish this material in the first place? The basic reason is, as was stated in our original reply to [Attorney General John] Mitchell, that we believe "that it is in the interest of the people of this country to be informed. . . ." A fundamental responsibility of the press in this democracy is to publish information that helps the people of the United States to understand the processes of their own government, especially when those processes have been clouded over in a hazy veil of public dissimulation [false appearances] and even deception. . . .

The documents in question belong to history. They refer to the development of American interest and participation in Indochina from the post-World War II period up to mid-1968, which is now almost three years ago. Their publication could not conceivably damage American security interests, much less the lives of Americans or Indochinese. We therefore felt it incumbent [required] to take on ourselves the responsibility for their publication. . . .

We publish the documents and related running account not to prove any debator's point about the origins and development of American participation in the war, not to place the finger of blame on any individuals, civilian or military, but to present to the American public a history—admittedly incomplete—of decision-making at the highest levels of government on one of the most vital issues that has ever affected "our lives, our fortunes and our sacred honor"—an issue on which the American people and their duly elected representatives in Congress have been largely curtained off from the truth.

It is the effort to expose and elucidate [explain] that truth that is the very essence of freedom of the press.

—*From "The Vietnam Documents,"* The New York Times, *June 16, 1971.*

## THINK ABOUT THIS

1. What reasons does the *Times* give for publishing the Pentagon Papers?
2. The *Times* quotes from what may be the most important document in American history. The words "our lives, our fortunes and our sacred honor" are from the Declaration of Independence. By evoking the sentiments of the Declaration in this indirect way, what message are the editors sending to government leaders?

## President Nixon Wields a "Smoking Gun"

Following the publication of the Pentagon Papers, President Nixon ordered his aides to create a secret White House unit, nicknamed the "plumbers," to plug "leaks" of government secrets. On June 17, 1972, the plumbers were caught breaking into Democratic Party headquarters at the Watergate Building in Washington, D.C., to bug the phones. That break-in and the administration's attempts to cover it up became known as the Watergate scandal. The most damaging evidence of Nixon's involvement in Watergate came from his own mouth, in conversations captured by a tape-recording system in the Oval Office. The following conversation was recorded a few days after the break-in. The president and his chief of staff, H. R. Haldeman, are concerned that FBI investigators might discover that money illegally donated to the Nixon reelection campaign was used to finance the plumbers' operations. The recording, which has been called the "smoking gun" tape, proved that Nixon was involved in the cover-up from the start. On August 9, 1974, facing the threat of impeachment for his role in Watergate, Nixon became the first U.S. president to resign from office.

*JUNE 23, 1972, 10:04 TO 11:39 A.M.*

*" . . . don't lie to them to the extent to say there is no involvement."*

HALDEMAN: Now, on the investigation, you know, the Democratic break-in thing, we're back in the problem area because the FBI is not under control, because [FBI Director Pat] Gray doesn't exactly know how to control them, and they have—their investigation is now leading into some productive areas, because they've been able to trace the money . . . and it goes in some directions we don't want it to go. . . . [Attorney General John] Mitchell came up with yesterday—and [presidential legal counsel] John Dean analyzed very carefully last night and concurs now with Mitchell's recommendation—that the only way to solve this . . . is for us to have [CIA Deputy Director Vernon] Walters call Pat Gray and just say, "Stay the hell out of this. . . . This is, ah, business here, we don't want you to go any further on it." . . .

NIXON: What about Pat Gray, ah, you mean he doesn't want to?

HALDEMAN: Pat does want to. He doesn't know how to, and he doesn't have—he doesn't have any basis for doing it. Given this, he will then have the basis. . . .

NIXON: Good. Good deal! Play it tough. That's the way they play it and that's the way we are going to play it.

HALDEMAN: Okay. We'll do it. . . .

NIXON: When you get in these people [the CIA], when you . . . get these people in, say, "Look, . . . the President just feels that"—

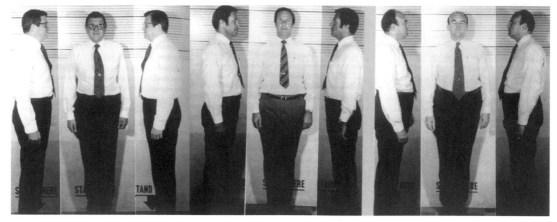

A most unusual primary source: "mug shots" of top White House officials arrested for their roles in the Watergate scandal. *From left to right:* special counsel Charles Colson, Chief of Staff H. R. Haldeman, and domestic affairs adviser John Ehrlichman.

ah, without going into the details—don't, don't lie to them to the extent to say there is no involvement, but just say this is sort of a comedy of errors, bizarre, without getting into it, . . . that they should call the FBI in and say that we wish for the country, don't go any further into this case, period!

HALDEMAN: Okay.

NIXON: That's the way to put it, do it straight.

—From "Richard Nixon and H. R. Haldeman Watergate White House 'Smoking Gun' Tape," "History and Politics Out Loud," at http://www.hpol.org/record.asp?id=92

## THINK ABOUT THIS

**1.** Why do you think this recording was so damaging to Nixon's hold on the presidency?

**2.** Why do you think it is called the "smoking gun" tape?

## Doonesbury Draws on Watergate

Political cartoonists had a field day with the bizarre twists and turns of Watergate: the bungling burglars, the secret tapes, the Nixon administration's tangled web of half-truths and lies. Garry Trudeau's comic strip *Doonesbury* blended political commentary and cartoon humor as it chronicled the unfolding scandal. *Doonesbury* was carried by more than 350 North American newspapers and widely read by decision makers in the nation's capital. In fact, President Gerald Ford, who took office after Nixon's resignation, said, "There are only three major vehicles to keep us informed as to what is going on in Washington: the electronic media, the print media, and *Doonesbury,* not necessarily in that order." In this cartoon Nixon and a legal adviser chat inside the White House about Watergate.

—From G. B. Trudeau, The Doonesbury Chronicles.
New York: Holt, Rinehart and Winston, 1975.

## THINK ABOUT THIS

1. Columnist Garry Wills praised Trudeau's "economy of drawing." How and why do you think Trudeau uses that "economy" in this cartoon?

2. Why do you think a comic strip became "must reading" for politicians in Washington?

A veteran at the Vietnam Memorial Moving Wall, a traveling reproduction of the Vietnam Veterans Memorial in Washington, D.C. The memorials bear the names of the more than 58,000 servicemen and women killed or missing in action in Vietnam.

# Chapter 9

# Coming Home

**A**FTER 1970 THERE WAS little talk of victory in Vietnam. The U.S. government's main goal had become Vietnamization—getting its troops out while shifting the responsibility of fighting to the South Vietnamese. President Nixon had ordered the first troop withdrawals in June 1969. By December of that year, 475,000 servicemen and women remained in Vietnam—the lowest number since 1967. By the end of 1970, 334,600 troops remained; by the end of 1971, only 157,000.

Americans usually served for a one-year tour of duty in Vietnam. That meant that even as troops were withdrawn, soldiers continued to arrive in the country to replace some of those going home. For these new arrivals, Vietnam was more of a nightmare than ever. They were fighting an unpopular war, for a cause hardly anyone believed in anymore. Short of manpower, their platoons were often sent into the field at half-strength or less. Increasingly, troops refused to obey orders, especially in enemy territory—no one wanted to be "the last American to die in Vietnam." Some combat leaders abandoned attempts to seek out the enemy and destroy targets, instead taking their men on "search-and-evade" missions, with the main objective of getting everyone back safely. Unpopular commanders—those who were seen as incompetent or overaggressive, and so a threat to survival—were sometimes threatened, sometimes even killed by their own men. Drug and alcohol use among the troops skyrocketed. Racial incidents abounded. In June 1971 a retired marine officer warned, "Our army that now remains in Vietnam is in a state approaching collapse."

As the war dragged on and troop withdrawals continued, President Nixon's national security adviser, Henry Kissinger, was holding secret talks with North Vietnamese negotiators in Paris. In early 1973 the two sides reached an agreement. On January 27, 1973, the United States, North Vietnam, and South Vietnam signed the Paris Peace Accords, officially ending U.S. military involvement in Vietnam.

The government of South Vietnam lasted a little more than two years after U.S. withdrawal. On April 30, 1975, Communist troops rolled into Saigon and raised the flag of North Vietnam over the presidential palace. The long war had finally come to an end.

More than 58,000 Americans died during the Vietnam War. Another 300,000 were wounded, and about 2,000 are still listed as missing in action. No one knows how many Vietnamese soldiers and civilians were killed, but estimates range as high as two million. The Vietnamese people continued to suffer for many years following the war, from the poverty and destruction left behind.

The Vietnam War years left a lasting legacy in the United States as well. The era's commitment to social change led to great strides in civil rights for African Americans and equal rights for women, as well as a greater tolerance for differences in dress and lifestyle. The credibility gap led Americans to more freely question, criticize, and challenge their leaders. And the country's first loss in war resulted in what is still called the "Vietnam syndrome"—a reluctance to send U.S. troops to fight in foreign conflicts unless the goals are clear and the country is united behind the cause.

## Three Servicemen Return Home from Vietnam

Americans came home from Vietnam a few at a time, as their one-year tours ended, and in larger groups at the war's end. Often their homecoming experience was a shock. Instead of gratitude for their service, many veterans were greeted with indifference or even hostility. Some Americans wanted to forget the disastrous war had ever happened. Others seemed to blame the veterans for America's policy in Vietnam or to believe that every serviceman had committed atrocities like the My Lai massacre. When newspaper columnist Bob Greene invited veterans to tell him about their first encounters on U.S. soil, he received more than a thousand letters. These three accounts reflect the range of reactions to servicemen returning from America's most controversial war.

*Scott Brooks-Miller, Spokane, Washington*
I returned from Vietnam in July of 1970 after a year in country with the 12th and 11th Marines. We flew into Norton Air Force Base in Southern California. . . . After saying our farewells, I went to the terminal in which I would catch my flight back to Illinois (I'm from Peoria).

While walking down the corridor, I encountered a young man, no older than myself I'm sure, who looked me in the eye and without hesitation spit on my ribbons. I didn't know what to do. I still don't. For all these years I've remembered that experience.

Yes, I'm bitter, and probably always will be. We were not politicians—most of us couldn't even vote. We simply did what we were asked to do, just as our fathers and grandfathers and all the generations preceding did. But because it was an unpopular war, we took the brunt of the anger of the American people. I was spit on and that moment in time came to symbolize to me the way the American people felt about me.

*Jim Sorensen, McKinleyville, California*
I will tell you what happened to me and another GI on a United flight from San Francisco to Fresno via San Jose. The flight we were on was less than half full, but the stewardess tactfully told us the plane was short on meals in coach, and asked if we would please move into the first class section. The other soldier and I became the only first class passengers on the plane.

I will never forget this woman's kindness, because it was my welcome home to "The World" after 22 months away.

Contrast this to something which happened a couple of days later at home, a small San Joaquin Valley town near Fresno. I walked into a bar, whose owner and proprietor was a neighbor and lifelong family acquaintance. He greeted me, "Hi, Jim. Still working in the woods?" (I should explain that I was a logger before enlisting in the Army in 1966.) What a fine greeting after being gone for nearly two years, especially considering the source.

The point is, I could have dealt with spit. I had, and still have, a hell of a time dealing with the indifference I met upon coming home.

*Bob Boughton, Fredericktown, Ohio*
I have a true story that involves a "hippie."

I was recovering from injuries received in Vietnam at a military hospital near Philadelphia. While waiting for a bus home there, an elderly woman came up to me, looked me square in the face, and called me a hired killer.

But as I said, my story included a "hippie." A young lady dressed in bell-bottoms, love beads, and a peace symbol came up to me as the elderly woman walked away. She looked me in the face and told me she was sorry for the way the returning vets were being treated.

I never got the chance to thank her, nor even got her name. But I could never forget her face and those few kind words.

—From Bob Greene, Homecoming: When the Soldiers Returned from Vietnam.
New York: G. P. Putnam's, 1989.

## THINK ABOUT THIS

1. What do these accounts tell you about the mood of the American people during the Vietnam War?
2. Which of the incidents described here surprises you the most? Why? How can you explain the actions of the person(s) involved?

# The Paris Peace Accords End U.S. Involvement in Vietnam

Formal negotiations to end the Vietnam War began in May 1968, under the Johnson administration. A year later, frustrated by the lack of progress, President Nixon sent his national security adviser, Henry Kissinger, to hold secret talks with the North Vietnamese in Paris. Those talks dragged on for more than three years. Finally, in January 1973, the two sides settled on terms for a peace agreement. The Paris Peace Accords called for a cease-fire, the withdrawal of U.S. troops from Vietnam, and the release of all American prisoners of war. North Vietnam's forces would remain in the South while an international council was set up to work out a permanent peace settlement and reunite the country. At first, Nguyen Van Thieu, who had been elected South Vietnam's president in 1967, rejected the agreement, accusing the United States of abandoning his country to the Communists. But when Nixon threatened a complete cutoff of U.S. military and economic aid, Thieu was forced to agree. On January 27, 1973, the Paris Peace Accords were signed, ending U.S. involvement in Vietnam. Following are some of the key provisions of the agreement.

### ARTICLE 1
The United States and all other countries respect the independence, sovereignty, unity, and territorial integrity of Vietnam as recognized by the 1954 Geneva Agreements on Vietnam. . . .

### ARTICLE 2
A cease-fire shall be observed throughout South Vietnam as of 2400 hours G.M.T. [Greenwich Mean Time], on January 27, 1973.

At the same hour, the United States will stop all its military activities against the territory of the Democratic Republic of Vietnam [North Vietnam] by ground, air and naval forces, wherever they may be based, and end the mining of the territorial waters, ports, harbors, and waterways of the Democratic Republic of Vietnam. . . .

### ARTICLE 3
The parties undertake to maintain the cease-fire and to ensure a lasting and stable peace. . . .

The armed forces of the two South Vietnamese parties [the governments of North and South Vietnam] shall remain in-place. . . .

*ARTICLE 4*

The United States will not continue its military involvement or intervene in the internal affairs of South Vietnam.

*ARTICLE 5*

Within sixty days of the signing of this Agreement, there will be a total withdrawal from South Vietnam of troops, military advisers, and military personnel . . . of the United States. . . .

*ARTICLE 6*

The dismantlement of all military bases in South Vietnam of the United States . . . shall be completed within sixty days of the signing of this Agreement. . . .

*ARTICLE 7*

. . . The two South Vietnamese parties shall not accept the introduction of troops, military advisers, and military personnel including technical military personnel, armaments, munitions, and war material into South Vietnam. . . .

*ARTICLE 8*

(a) The return of captured military personnel and foreign civilians of the parties shall be carried out simultaneously with and completed not later than the same day as the troop withdrawal mentioned in Article 5. The parties shall exchange complete lists of the above-mentioned captured military personnel and foreign civilians on the day of the signing of this Agreement.

(b) The Parties shall help each other to get information about those military personnel and foreign civilians of the parties missing in action.

*—From U.S. Secretary of State, compiler and editor,* United States Treaties and Other International Agreements, *vol. 24, part 1. Washington, D.C.: U. S. Government Printing Office, 1974.*

1. What does the agreement require each of the parties—the United States, North Vietnam, and South Vietnam—to do?
2. South Vietnamese General Cao Van Vien said that the Paris agreement "served only the immediate purposes of the United States and North Vietnam." Do you think the document supports that statement? How?

## A Navy Captain Describes the Evacuation of Saigon

The Paris Peace Accords did not bring peace to Vietnam. Although the agreement called for a cease-fire "in-place," it did not say where the armies of the north and south belonged. So each side fought on, trying to grab as much territory as possible before an international commission could be set up to oversee the truce. With U.S. financial aid drastically reduced, South Vietnam's economy collapsed. Its government became more corrupt and despised than ever, and its army shrank as many soldiers deserted. Then, in December 1974, the North Vietnamese Army launched an all-out offensive. NVA forces swiftly swept down from the north, capturing one stronghold after another as the South Vietnamese, soldiers and civilians alike, fled before them. By April 27, 1975, the Communists had reached the outskirts of Saigon. Mobbed with hundreds of thousands of refugees, the city was swept up in panic and confusion. U.S. ships, cargo planes, and helicopters evacuated the remaining Americans and as many of the desperate South Vietnamese as they could carry. In this official report, Captain R. E. Kemble, master of one of the navy evacuation ships, describes the chaotic scene on April 29, the day before North Vietnamese tanks rolled into Saigon.

ON THE 29TH AT 0700 HOURS it appeared as if an attack on Vung Tau [east of Saigon] was in progress. Large splashes observed in the water along shore and several explosions observed on shore in the resort section of the city. . . . Started loading refugees in increasing numbers. As the refugees would come aboard they would abandon their boats and let them drift off. Enemy action still going strong at Vung Tau so for the safety of all concerned, anchorage was shifted to 6 miles off of Vung Tau. We towed four fishing boats out with us and many more followed under their own power. At the anchorage, loading commenced immediately with all hands including security personnel now engaged in loading refugees. . . . By 1600 a continuous stream of vessels and anything else that would float were alongside the vessel and the crew loading them as fast as possible. At 1720 stopped loading refugees upon orders not to exceed 6000. Had to cut boats loose and steam. . . .

Desperate South Vietnamese climb the walls outside the U.S. Embassy in Saigon, trying to reach helicopters evacuating the last Americans as Communist troops close in on the capital, April 30, 1975.

At 1745 received orders from MSC [Military Sealift Command] Saigon to continue loading and to take up to 8000 refugees. Stopped the ship and shortly the boats that were following us caught up and we commenced embarking more refugees. At 1900 received orders from Saigon to load up to 10,000 refugees. At that time at least 80 boats were moored or milling alongside with hundreds streaming towards us. Refugees almost in panic stage trying to get on board. Loading refugees

Vietnamese "boat people," 1977. After the Communist takeover, thousands of Vietnamese tried to escape poverty and repression by fleeing their homeland in small boats. Many drowned or were killed by pirates in the South China Sea.

by cargo booms, ladders and nets. The sight was unbelievable. . . . At least 20 or more refugees in each cargo net . . . including women . . . with small babies in their arms hanging on to cargo nets with small children hanging on to their mothers—and still they come. The situation was pitiful, unbelievable and heart rending. . . . At 2000 hours we had to stop with an estimated 10,000 refugees on board and just no room for any others. 70 or 80 boats were still alongside and pleading with us to please take them and more boats still observed coming towards us. We had to cut boats loose in order to get away. It's a sight that will be impressed in everyone's memory for a long time. We did our best and yet it seemed so inadequate.

*—From Captain (U.S.N.) R. E. Kemble, Report to Commander, Subject: "Vietnam Sealift Evacuation History," July 24, 1975. Naval Historical Center, Washington, D.C.*

## THINK ABOUT THIS

1. What difficulties did U.S. military personnel encounter in the emergency pullout from Saigon?
2. Why do you think the evacuation was so chaotic?

# A Washington Memorial Honors Vietnam Veterans

In November 1982 the Vietnam Veterans Memorial was dedicated in Washington, D.C. A long, low wall made of seventy reflective black granite panels, the memorial is engraved with the names of the more than 58,000 Americans who did not make it home from Vietnam. The names appear chronologically, from the first servicemen who died in 1957 to the last Americans who fell during the evacuation of Saigon in 1975. The Wall has become one of the most visited sites in Washington, a place for remembering, grieving, and honoring those who gave their lives in Vietnam. Over the years visitors have left behind thousands of letters, poems, photos, and personal mementoes—flowers and wreaths, medals and combat boots, playing cards and teddy bears. Here are four of those messages of loss and remembrance.

*My son Ralphie:*
How I miss you! I want you to talk to me. I think of you every day and every hour of the day and night. If I could hug you and kiss you one more time. Oh Ralphie, how I miss you. There's no words for it. I love you my son. Be with God and I'll pray for you.
  *All our love,*
    *Mom, Dad, Amy and Karen*

Even though I never really knew you, you still meant the world to me. Thank you, Daddy, for giving me three years of your life. Remembering you through photos, I can only say I love you, Daddy. Happy Father's Day. Part of me died with you.
  *Love,*
    *Your son, Joe*

A veteran gives a very personal response to critics who disliked the simple, "modern-art" design of the Vietnam Veterans Memorial in Washington.

*My dearest Paul,*
I finally got here—a beautiful monument for you. I miss you, and I know you're watching over me. I love you,
    *Your wife*

This wedding ring belonged to a young Viet Cong fighter. He was killed by a Marine unit in the Phu Loc province of South Vietnam in May of 1968. I wish I knew more about this young man. I have carried this ring for 18 years and it's time for me to lay it down. This boy is not my enemy any longer.
    *Frederick Garten, Sgt. USMC*

—*From Laura Palmer,* Shrapnel in the Heart: Letters and Remembrances from the Vietnam Veterans Memorial. *New York: Random House, 1987.*

## THINK ABOUT THIS

1. A nationwide competition was held to choose the design for the Vietnam memorial, but some people objected to the judges' choice. You can get an idea of what the Wall looks like from the photo of its traveling replica on page 110. Which do you prefer—this type of contemporary memorial or more traditional statues of soldiers in heroic poses? Why?

2. The Wall's designer, a Chinese-American college student named Maya Lin, insisted that the memorial be made of black granite, so viewers could see their own reflection among the names of the fallen. Why do you think this was important to her design?

# Time Line

**NOVEMBER 8**
John F. Kennedy is elected thirty-fifth president of the United States.

**FEBRUARY 12**
The United States sends advisers to train the South Vietnamese army.

**MAY 7**
Ho Chi Minh's Vietnamese Communists defeat the French at Dien Bien Phu.

**APRIL 4**
President Dwight Eisenhower pledges to maintain South Vietnam as a separate state

1 9 5 4       1 9 5 5       1 9 5 9       1 9 6 0

U.S.-backed Ngo Dinh Diem becomes president of South Vietnam.

**OCTOBER 26**

The Geneva Conference calls for a cease-fire and divides Vietnam, with Ho Chi Minh leading in the north and Bao Dai in the south.

**JULY 21**

North Vietnamese Communist leaders form the National Liberation Front to overthrow the government of South Vietnam.

**DECEMBER 20**

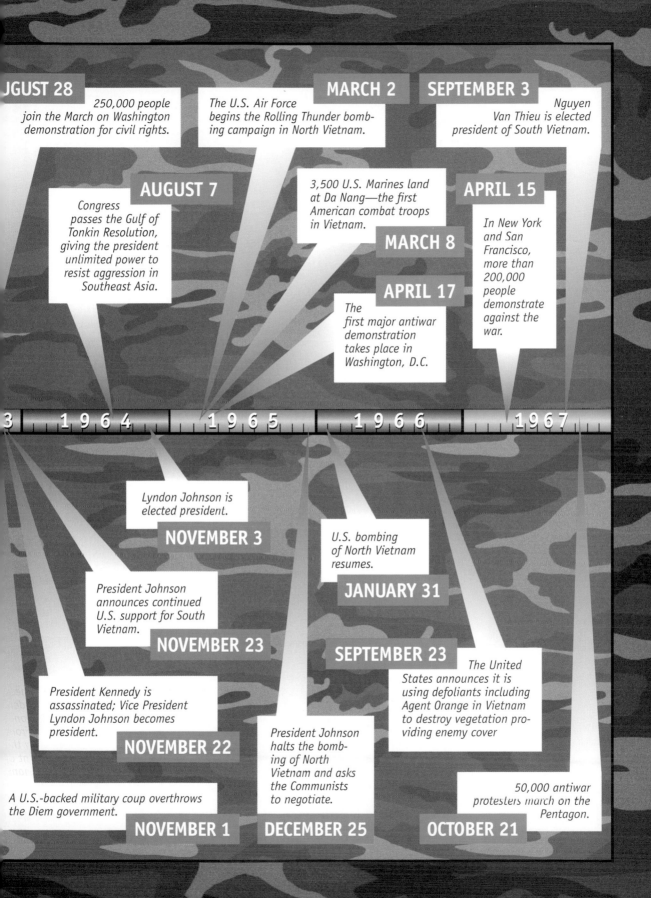

**JGUST 28**
250,000 people join the March on Washington demonstration for civil rights.

**MARCH 2**
The U.S. Air Force begins the Rolling Thunder bombing campaign in North Vietnam.

**SEPTEMBER 3**
Nguyen Van Thieu is elected president of South Vietnam.

**AUGUST 7**
Congress passes the Gulf of Tonkin Resolution, giving the president unlimited power to resist aggression in Southeast Asia.

3,500 U.S. Marines land at Da Nang—the first American combat troops in Vietnam.

**MARCH 8**

**APRIL 15**
In New York and San Francisco, more than 200,000 people demonstrate against the war.

**APRIL 17**
The first major antiwar demonstration takes place in Washington, D.C.

**3   1 9 6 4   1 9 6 5   1 9 6 6   1 9 6 7**

Lyndon Johnson is elected president.

**NOVEMBER 3**

U.S. bombing of North Vietnam resumes.

**JANUARY 31**

President Johnson announces continued U.S. support for South Vietnam.

**NOVEMBER 23**

**SEPTEMBER 23**
The United States announces it is using defoliants including Agent Orange in Vietnam to destroy vegetation providing enemy cover

President Kennedy is assassinated; Vice President Lyndon Johnson becomes president.

**NOVEMBER 22**

President Johnson halts the bombing of North Vietnam and asks the Communists to negotiate.

50,000 antiwar protesters march on the Pentagon.

A U.S.-backed military coup overthrows the Diem government.

**NOVEMBER 1**

**DECEMBER 25**

**OCTOBER 21**

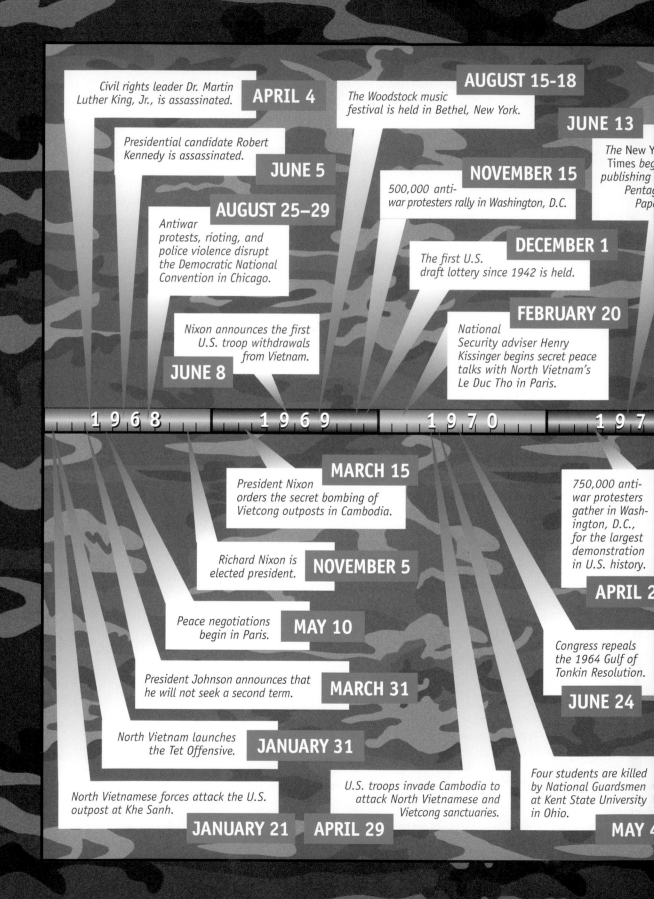

Civil rights leader Dr. Martin Luther King, Jr., is assassinated.
**APRIL 4**

The Woodstock music festival is held in Bethel, New York.
**AUGUST 15-18**

**JUNE 13**

The New Y
Times beg
publishing
Pentag
Pap

Presidential candidate Robert Kennedy is assassinated.
**JUNE 5**

500,000 anti-war protesters rally in Washington, D.C.
**NOVEMBER 15**

**AUGUST 25–29**

Antiwar protests, rioting, and police violence disrupt the Democratic National Convention in Chicago.

The first U.S. draft lottery since 1942 is held.
**DECEMBER 1**

**FEBRUARY 20**

National Security adviser Henry Kissinger begins secret peace talks with North Vietnam's Le Duc Tho in Paris.

Nixon announces the first U.S. troop withdrawals from Vietnam.
**JUNE 8**

**1 9 6 8**   **1 9 6 9**   **1 9 7 0**   **1 9 7**

**MARCH 15**

President Nixon orders the secret bombing of Vietcong outposts in Cambodia.

750,000 anti-war protesters gather in Wash-ington, D.C., for the largest demonstration in U.S. history.
**APRIL 2**

Richard Nixon is elected president.
**NOVEMBER 5**

Peace negotiations begin in Paris.
**MAY 10**

Congress repeals the 1964 Gulf of Tonkin Resolution.
**JUNE 24**

President Johnson announces that he will not seek a second term.
**MARCH 31**

North Vietnam launches the Tet Offensive.
**JANUARY 31**

North Vietnamese forces attack the U.S. outpost at Khe Sanh.
**JANUARY 21**

U.S. troops invade Cambodia to attack North Vietnamese and Vietcong sanctuaries.
**APRIL 29**

Four students are killed by National Guardsmen at Kent State University in Ohio.
**MAY 4**

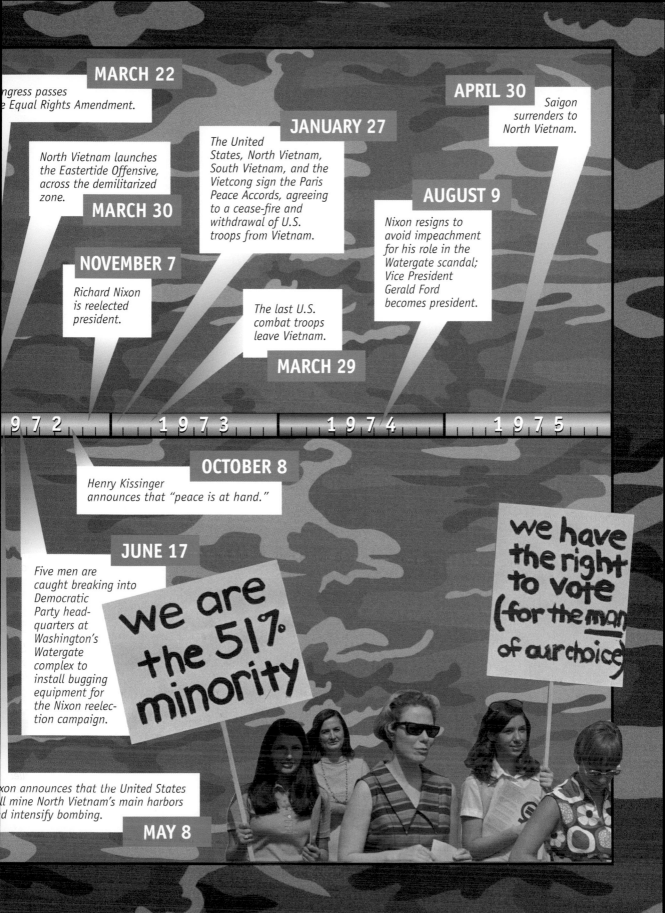

**MARCH 22**

ngress passes
e Equal Rights Amendment.

North Vietnam launches
the Eastertide Offensive,
across the demilitarized
zone.

**MARCH 30**

**JANUARY 27**

The United
States, North Vietnam,
South Vietnam, and the
Vietcong sign the Paris
Peace Accords, agreeing
to a cease-fire and
withdrawal of U.S.
troops from Vietnam.

**APRIL 30**

Saigon
surrenders to
North Vietnam.

**AUGUST 9**

Nixon resigns to
avoid impeachment
for his role in the
Watergate scandal;
Vice President
Gerald Ford
becomes president.

**NOVEMBER 7**

Richard Nixon
is reelected
president.

The last U.S.
combat troops
leave Vietnam.

**MARCH 29**

**9 7 2**     **1 9 7 3**     **1 9 7 4**     **1 9 7 5**

**OCTOBER 8**

Henry Kissinger
announces that "peace is at hand."

**JUNE 17**

Five men are
caught breaking into
Democratic
Party head-
quarters at
Washington's
Watergate
complex to
install bugging
equipment for
the Nixon reelec-
tion campaign.

we are
the 51%
minority

we have
the right
to vote
(for the man
of our choice)

xon announces that the United States
ll mine North Vietnam's main harbors
d intensify bombing.

**MAY 8**

# Glossary

**alienation** withdrawal or separation from a person or society

**amphibious** able to operate on land or water

**ARVN** the Army of the Republic of [South] Vietnam

**attrition** slowly wearing down enemy forces through constant harassment and attacks

**beleaguered** surrounded by enemy forces

**catatonia** inability to move

**conflagration** a large fire

**domino theory** the idea that if one of the nations of Southeast Asia fell to Communist power, the others would topple like a row of dominoes

**escalate** to expand a war by committing additional forces, increasing the intensity of fighting, or widening the areas of combat

**evac hospital** a military hospital for seriously wounded patients awaiting "evacuation" to hospitals outside the country

**firefight** a brief but fierce exchange of fire between enemies

**GI** a member of the U.S. armed forces; from "government issue," referring to uniforms and other items issued to soldiers by the military

**guerrilla** (pronounced like "gorilla") a type of fighting or fighter that uses surprise and stealth instead of direct combat to wear down a better-equipped opponent

**hierarchy** an organized group of people in authority

**Indochina** the region that included Vietnam, Cambodia, and Laos

**infantrymen** the foot soldiers of an army

**militant** aggressively active in a cause

**napalm** a jellied compound made mainly of gasoline, which is loaded in bombs and dropped from airplanes to cause widespread fires

**NVA** the North Vietnamese Army, which often fought alongside the Vietcong; also, a soldier in that army

**propaganda** ideas spread to further one's cause; half truths

**Purple Heart** a medal awarded to GIs wounded in action

**radical** extreme; also, a person who favors extreme changes or reforms

**Ranger companies** soldiers specially trained for operations deep in enemy territory

**sabotage** secret damage or destruction carried out to interfere with an enemy's ability to make war

**sovereignty** right of self-government; freedom from external control

**Vietcong** guerrillas who worked to overthrow the government of South Vietnam; also called VC, Victor, or Charlie

**Vietnamization** President Richard Nixon's policy of gradually withdrawing U.S. combat troops from Vietnam while shifting the burden of fighting to South Vietnamese troops

# To Find Out More

## BOOKS

Archer, Jules. *The Incredible Sixties: The Stormy Years That Changed America.* San Diego, CA: Harcourt Brace Jovanovich, 1986.

Brown, Gene. *The Nation in Turmoil: Civil Rights and the Vietnam War (1960-1973).* New York: Henry Holt, 1993.

Denenberg, Barry. *Voices from Vietnam.* New York: Scholastic, 1995.

Dougan, Clark, Samuel Lipsman, and the editors of Boston Publishing Company. *A Nation Divided.* Boston: Boston Publishing Company, 1984.

Dudley, William, ed. *The Vietnam War: Opposing Viewpoints.* San Diego, CA: Greenhaven Press, 1998.

Edmonds, Anthony O. *The War in Vietnam.* Westport, CT: Greenwood Press, 1998.

Gay, Kathlyn, and Martin Gay. *Vietnam War.* New York: Henry Holt, 1996.

Hoobler, Dorothy, and Thomas Hoobler. *Vietnam: Why We Fought.* New York: Alfred A. Knopf, 1990.

Marrin, Albert. *America and Vietnam: The Elephant and the Tiger.* New York: Viking, 1992.

Schomp, Virginia. *The Vietnam War.* Letters from the Homefront series. New York: Benchmark Books, 2002.

———. *The Vietnam War.* Letters from the Battlefront series. New York: Benchmark Books, 2003.

Summers, Henry G., Jr. *Vietnam War Almanac.* New York: Facts on File, 1985.

Tucker, Spencer C., ed. *The Encyclopedia of the Vietnam War: A Political, Social, and Military History.* New York: Oxford University Press, 1998.

Wright, David K. *Causes and Consequences of the Vietnam War.* Austin, TX: Raintree Steck-Vaughn, 1996.

———. *A Multicultural Portrait of the Vietnam War.* New York: Benchmark Books, 1996.

Zeinert, Karen. *The Valiant Women of the Vietnam War.* Brookfield, CT: Millbrook Press, 2000.

## VIDEO

*Vietnam: A Television History.* Written by Andrew Pearson. Produced by WGBH Education Foundation, Boston, 1983. Distributed by Sony Video Software Company.

## WEBSITES

The websites listed here were in existence in 2003–2004 when this book was being written. Their names and/or locations may have changed since then.

In general, when using the Internet to do research on a history topic, you should use caution. You will find numerous websites that are very attractive to look at and appear to be professional in format. Proceed with caution, however. Many, even the best ones, contain errors. Some websites even insert disclaimers or warnings about mistakes that may have made their way into the site. In the case of primary sources, the builders of the website often transcribe previously published material, good or bad, accurate or inaccurate. Therefore, you have to judge the content of *all* websites. This requires a critical eye.

A good rule for using the Internet as a resource is always to compare what you find in websites to several other sources such as librarian- or teacher-recommended reference works and major works of scholarship. By doing this, you will discover the many different versions of history that exist.

"The American Experience: Vietnam Online" at
**http://www.pbs.org/wgbh/amex/vietnam**

"Battlefield Vietnam" at **http://www.pbs.org/battlefieldvietnam**

"History and Politics Out Loud" at **http://www.hpol.org**

"LBJ White House Tapes" at **http://www.c-span.org/lbj**

"National Civil Rights Museum" at **http://www.civilrightsmuseum.org**

"New Jersey Vietnam Veterans' Memorial Foundation" at
**http://www.njvvmf.org**

"Vietnam: A Country Study" at **http://lcweb2.loc.gov/frd/cs/vntoc.html**

"Vietnam: Then & Now" at
**http://thinkquest.org/library/lib/site_sum.html?lib_id=1617**

"The Virtual Wall: A Digital Legacy for Remembrance" at
**http://www.thevirtualwall.org**

# Index

Page numbers for illustrations are in boldface

Adams, Eddie, 7–9, **8**
African Americans
    Black Panthers, 75–78
    civil rights movement, **68**, 69–71
    Malcolm X speaks out against integration,
        73–75, **75**
    Martin Luther King's opposition to Vietnam
        War, 71–73, **72**
    racial tensions in the infantry, 80–81, **80**
    why black Americans should not serve in
        Vietnam, 78–79
    and women's liberation movement, 85–86
*Akron Beacon Journal*, 35, **36**, 37
American youth and the counterculture, 52, **53**,
    54–55, 57
    disillusionment of college students, 58–60, **59**
    generation gap poll, 62–64
    the "People's Park", 60–62
    Students for a Democratic Society, 55–57
    Woodstock, 54, 64–67, **66**
antiwar movement at home
    anthem of the antiwar movement, 65–66
    antiwar petitions, 29, **30**, 31
    Chicago rioters, 31–34, **34**
    and counterculture movement, 54
    Democratic National Convention, 1968,
        31, **34**
    doves for peace, 24, **25**, 26–27
    GI explains the war to American schoolchildren,
        43–44
    hawks for war, 38, **39**, 40
    and Kent State tragedy, 35, **36**, 37
    Martin Luther King's opposition to Vietnam
        War, 71–73, **72**
    President Johnson and U.S. involvement in
        Vietnam, xx–xxi, **xx**, 40–43, **42**, 99–102, **101**
    the "silent majority", 44–49, **48**
    U.S. soldiers and, 27–29, 49–51
antiwar protests, 24, **25**, 26
Army of the Republic of Vietnam (ARVN), xviii,
    xix, xxi
Arnett, Peter, 3–5
Associated Press (AP), 3, 8

attrition, war of, 12, 14
*Autobiography of Malcolm X, The* (Haley),
    74–75

baby boomers, **xiv**, xv, 52
Black Muslims, 73–74
Black Panther Party, 68, 75–78
Black Power movement, **68**, 70, 71, 76, 80, **80**
body counts, 14–15
booby traps and land mines, 14, 18–19
Boughton, Bob, 114–115
Brooks-Miller, Scott, 113–114
*Brown Daily Herald* (Brown University),
    58–60, **59**

Calley, William, 102
Carmichael, Stokely, 71
Cartinhour, John, Jr., 47–49
*CBS Evening News*, 10
*Chicago Sun-Times*, 31–34
civil rights bill, 71
civil rights movement, **68**, 69–71
    Black Panthers, 75–78
    Malcolm X speaks out against integration,
        73–75, **75**
    Martin Luther King's opposition to Vietnam
        War, 71–73, **72**
    racial tensions in the infantry, 80–81, **80**
    why black Americans should not serve in
        Vietnam, 78–79
Cold War, xvi
college campuses
    demonstrations on, **xxiii**, 55, **63**
    disillusionment of college students, 58–60, **59**
    Kent State University tragedy, 35, **36**, 37
    "People's Park", Berkeley, CA, 60–62
communism, xvi, xviii–xix, xxi, 43, 98, 116
Constitution, U.S.
    Equal Rights Amendment, 87–90
    Nineteenth Amendment, 85
correspondents, Vietnam-era war, 3–5, 10–11
counterculture movement. *see* American youth
    and the counterculture

credibility gap, 96, **97**, 98
  My Lai Massacre, 102–104
  Pentagon Papers, 104–106
  President Johnson and the Vietnam War, 99–102, **101**
Cronkite, Walter, 10–11

Democratic National Convention, 1968, 31, **34**
Diem, Ngo Dinh, xviii, 96
Dien Bien Phu, xvi
domino theory, xviii
*Doonesbury* (comic strip), 109, **109**
doves for peace (antiwar activists), 24, **25**, 26–27
drug and alcohol abuse
  among U.S. troops, 112
  by the counterculture, 54

Ehrhart, William, 22–23
Eisenhower, Dwight D., xviii
Ellsberg, Daniel, 104
Equal Rights Amendment (ERA), 84, 87–90
  anti-ERA groups, 90–92, **91**

*Feminine Mystique, The* (Friedan), 84
feminists, 83, 84–85, 88–90
Fitzpatrick, Tom, 31–34
flower children, 54
Ford, Gerald, 109
Ford, Richard, 80–81
Freedom Democratic Party, 78–79
freedom rides, 69
Friedan, Betty, 84, 85, 88

generation gap, 54–55
  *Life* magazine poll examines the, 62–64
Geneva peace agreements, xvi, xviii
Great Society programs, 41, 70
Greene, Bob, 113–115
*Greenfield Recorder* (Massachusetts), 50–51
grunts (American infantrymen), 14, 15, 18
"Guerrilla War" (poem), 22–23

Halderman, H. R., 106–108, **108**
Haley, Alex, 74–75
hawks for war (war supporters), 38, **39**, 40
Hayden, Tom, 55–57
Hersh, Seymour M., 102–103
hippies, **48**, 52, 54
Ho Chi Minh, xvi, xviii, xix

"I-Feel-Like-I'm-Fixin'-to-Die-Rag" (song), 65–66
integration, Malcolm X's opposition to, 73–75, **75**

Jackman, Robert B., 43–44
Johnson, Lyndon B., xix, xx–xxi, **xx**, 10, 24, 40–43, 44, 70, 98, 99–102, **101**
journalists, Vietnam-era
  and the credibility gap, 96, 98
  moments captured on photographs, 7–9, **8**, **17**
  newspaper journalists, 3–7, 7, 31–34, **34**, 35, **36**, 37, 104–106, 113–115
  television journalists, 2, 10–11

Kemble, R. E., 118–120
Kennedy, Florynce, 85–86
Kennedy, John F., xix, xviii, 40, 52, 70
Kennedy, Robert, 52
Kent State University, tragedy at, 35, **36**, 37
Khe Sanh, siege of, 20–21, **20**
King, Martin Luther, Jr., 27, 52, 69, 70, 71–73, **72**, 80
Kissinger, Henry, 112, 115
Korean War, 1, 2

land mines, 14, 18–19
*Life* magazine
  generation gap poll, 62–64
  women's liberation movement, 85–86
Lowndes County Freedom Organization, 76–77
Lusco, Gregory, 50–51

McDonald, Joe, 65–66
Malcolm X, 73–75, **75**
March on Washington, 69, 71
Marine, Corps, U.S., Supply Column 21 news story, 3–5
military advisers, U.S., **17**
*Ms.* (magazine), 88
My Lai Massacre, 102–104, 113

Nation of Islam, 73
National Guardsmen, 26, 31, 35
National Organization for Women (NOW), 84–85
National Women's Political Caucus, 88
*New York Times*, 54, 66, 98, 104–106
Nguyen Van Thieu, 116
Nineteenth Amendment, 85
Nixon, Richard M., xxi, 24, 35, 44–47, **97**, 98, 104, 106–108, 111, 115, 116
nonviolence movement, 70, 71
North Vietnamese Army (NVA), xx, xxii
nurses, military, 93–95, **94**

O'Brien, Tim, 18–19
Obst, David, 60–62
Olsen, George, 15–18
Olsen, Gregory, 102–103

pacifists, 26
Paris Peace Accords, xxii, 112, 115–118
peace rallies, 38, **39**, 40
Pentagon Papers, 98, 104–106
photographs, moments captured on, 7–9, **8**, **17**
poet, Vietnam veteran, 22–23
*Power of the Positive Woman, The* (Schlafly), 91–92
Pulitzer Prize
    for International Correspondence, 3
    winning photograph of assassination, 7–9, **8**

*Rolling Stone* magazine, 64–65

Sandecki, Rose, 93–95
Schlafly, Phyllis, 90–92, **91**
segregation, 69, 71
silent majority, the, 44–49, **48**
"smoking gun" tape, Nixon's, 107–108
soldiers, U.S.
    and antiwar movement, 27–29, 49–51
    black combat troops, 78–79, **80**
    booby traps and mines, 14, 18–19
    casualties, 98, 112
    drug and alcohol abuse among, 112
    explains the war to American schoolchildren, 43–44
    homecoming, 113–115
    on jungle patrols, 14, 15–18
    killed in Vietnam, xxi, 112
    missing in action, 112
    morale, physical, and psychological problems of, 111–112
    and My Lai Massacre, 102–104, 113
    new arrivals, 111

Operation Rolling Thunder, xx–xxi, 99

President Johnson and U.S. involvement in Vietnam, xx–xxi, **xx**, 40–43, **42**, 99–102, **101**
    racial tensions among, 80–81, **80**, 112
    on search-and-destroy missions, 14, 80
    in siege of Khe Sanh, 20–21, **20**
    troop withdrawals, 111–113, 115
    veterans memorial, **110**, 121–123, **122**

Sorensen, Jim, 114
South Vietnam, **xxiv**
    army troops, **17**
    attack on Khe Sanh, 20–21, **20**
    Diem's government, xviii, xix
    evacuation of Saigon, xxii, 118–120, **119**, **120**
    My Lai Massacre, 102–104, 113
    news coverage of, 96, 98
    and Paris Peace Accords, 116
Steinberg, David, 20–21

Steinem, Gloria, 88–90
STOP ERA (anti-ERA group), 90–91
Student Non-Violent Coordinating Committee (SNCC), 68, 75–76, 78
Students for a Democratic Society (SDS), 55–57

teach-ins, 26
television war
    Peter Arnett joins American forces under fire, 3–5
    Vietnam as America's first, 1–3
    Walter Cronkite reports from Vietnam, 10–11
    *Washington Daily News* and Tet Offensive, 6–7, 7
Tet Offensive, 6–9, 7, **8**, 10, 24, 40, 98
Tonkin Gulf Resolution, xx
Trudeau, Garry, 108–109

University of California, Berkeley, 60–62

Viet Minh, xvi, xix
Vietcong, xx, 12, 14, 15, 18, 102
Vietnam
    America's longest war, xv–xxiii, **xx**, **xxiv**
    end of Vietnam War, xxii, 112–113
    evacuation of Saigon, xxii, 118–120, **119**, **120**
    Paris Peace Accords ending U.S. involvement in, 112, 115–118
    President Johnson and U.S. involvement in, xx–xxi, **xx**, 40–43, **42**, 99–102, **101**
    time line of Vietnam War events, 124–127
    the unseen enemy, 12, **13**, 14–23, **17**, **20**
Vietnam syndrome, 113
Vietnam Veterans Memorial, Washington, D.C., **110**, 121–122
Vietnamization policy, xxi, 44–47, 111

*Washington Daily News*, 6–7, 7
Watergate scandal, 97, 98, 106–109, **108**, **109**
Weathermen, the (radical group), 31
women's liberation movement, **82**, 83–85
    anti-ERA groups, 90–92, **91**
    Equal Rights Amendment, 87–90
    *Life* magazine and, 85–86
    opponents of the, 90–92, **91**
women serving in Vietnam, 92–95, **94**
Women's Strike for Equality Day demonstrations, 85
Woodall, Phillip, 27–29
Woodstock festival, 54, 64–67, **66**
World War II, xv, 2

youth, American. *see* American youth and the counterculture

## ABOUT THE AUTHOR

Virginia Schomp has written more than forty books on nonfiction topics including careers, ancient cultures, and American history. Her favorite part of writing is the reading and research that comes first. That was especially true with this title for the AMERICAN VOICES series, which offered an opportunity to learn more about the people who helped shape the world we live in today. Ms. Schomp lives in the Catskill Mountain region of New York with her husband, Richard, and their son, Chip.